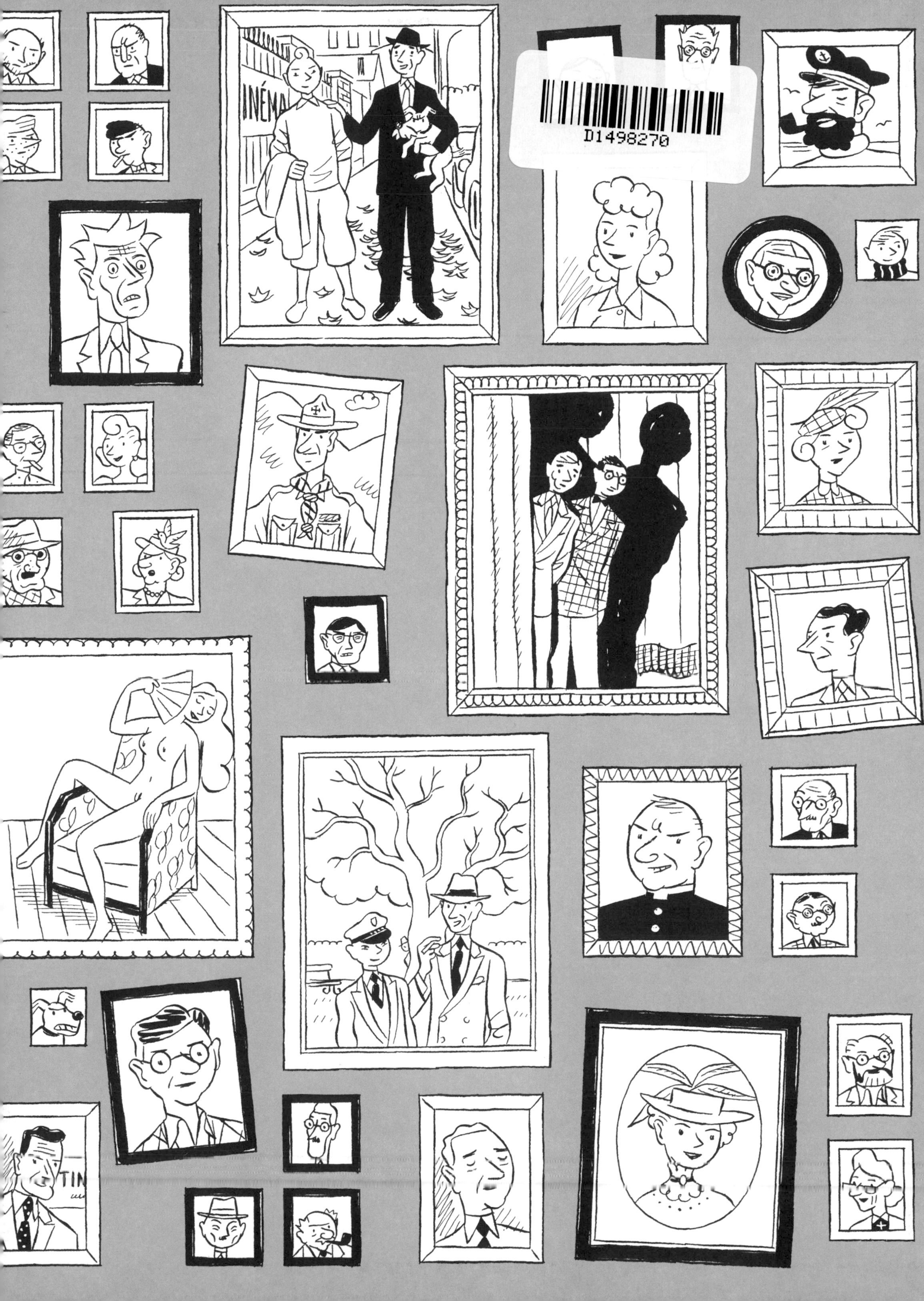

LINCOLN LIBRARY

March 2012   741.5

THE ADVENTURES OF HERGÉ

Lincoln Public Library
Lincoln Center, MA 01773

Drawn & Quarterly, Montréal

DEDICATED TO YVES BONIFACE.

Story copyright © 2011 José-Louis Bocquet and Jean-Luc Fromental. Illustrations copyright © 2011 Stanislas Barthélémy. All rights reserved. No part of this book (except small portions for review purposes) may be reproduced in any form without written permission from the artists or Drawn & Quarterly.

Published by arrangement with Editions Reporter. A slightly abridged version of this book was originally published in English in *Drawn & Quarterly Volume 4* (2001). Translation by Helge Dascher. Lettering by Dirk Rehm. Production assistance by Kimberly Tsui. Drawn & Quarterly acknowledges the financial contribution of the Government of Canada through the Canada Book Fund for our publishing activities and for support of this edition.

Drawn & Quarterly, Post Office Box 48056, Montréal, Québec, Canada H2V 4S8; drawnandquarterly.com.

First softcover edition: November 2011. Printed in Singapore. 10 9 8 7 6 5 4 3 2 1. Library and Archives Canada Cataloguing in Publication: Bocquet, José-Louis; *The Adventures of Hergé* / José-Louis Bocquet, Jean-Luc Fromental; illustrated by Stanislas Barthélémy; translated by Helge Dascher. Translation of: *Les Aventures d'Hergé*. ISBN 978-1-77046-059-1; 1. Hergé, 1907-1983—Comic books, strips, etc. 2. Cartoonists—Belgium—Biography—Comic books, strips, etc. I. Fromental, Jean-Luc; II. Stanislas; III. Title. PN6790.B43H47413 2011 741.5092 C2011-904059-X.

Distributed in the United States by Farrar, Straus & Giroux, 18 West 18th Street, New York, NY 10011; Orders: 888.330.8477. Distributed in Canada by Raincoast Books, 2440 Viking Way, Richmond, BC V6V 1N2; Orders: 800.663.5714.

THE ADVENTURES OF HERGÉ

Written by
José-Louis Bocquet *and*
Jean-Luc Fromental
Illustrated by
Stanislas Barthélémy
Translated by Helge Dascher

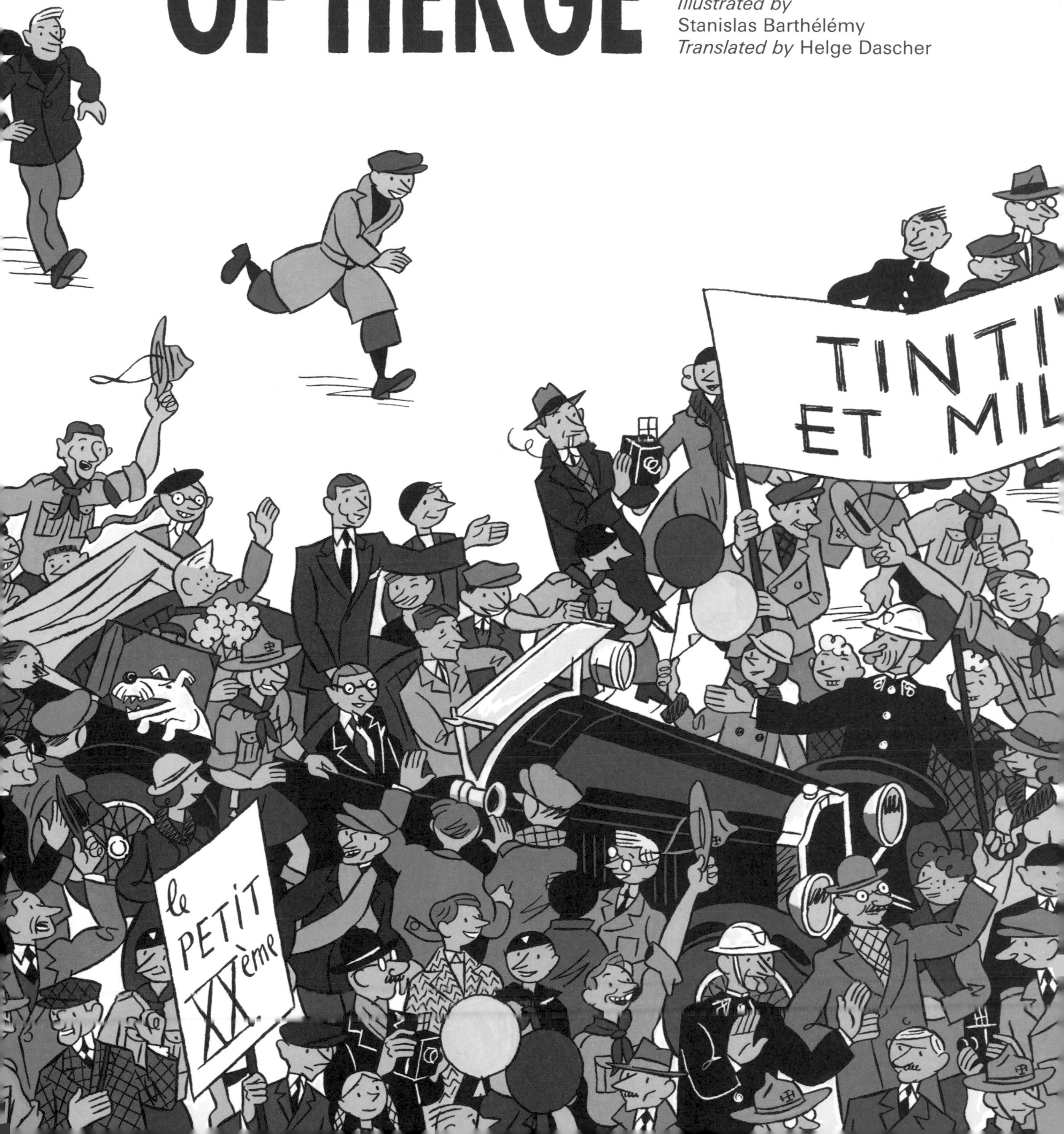
le PETIT XXème

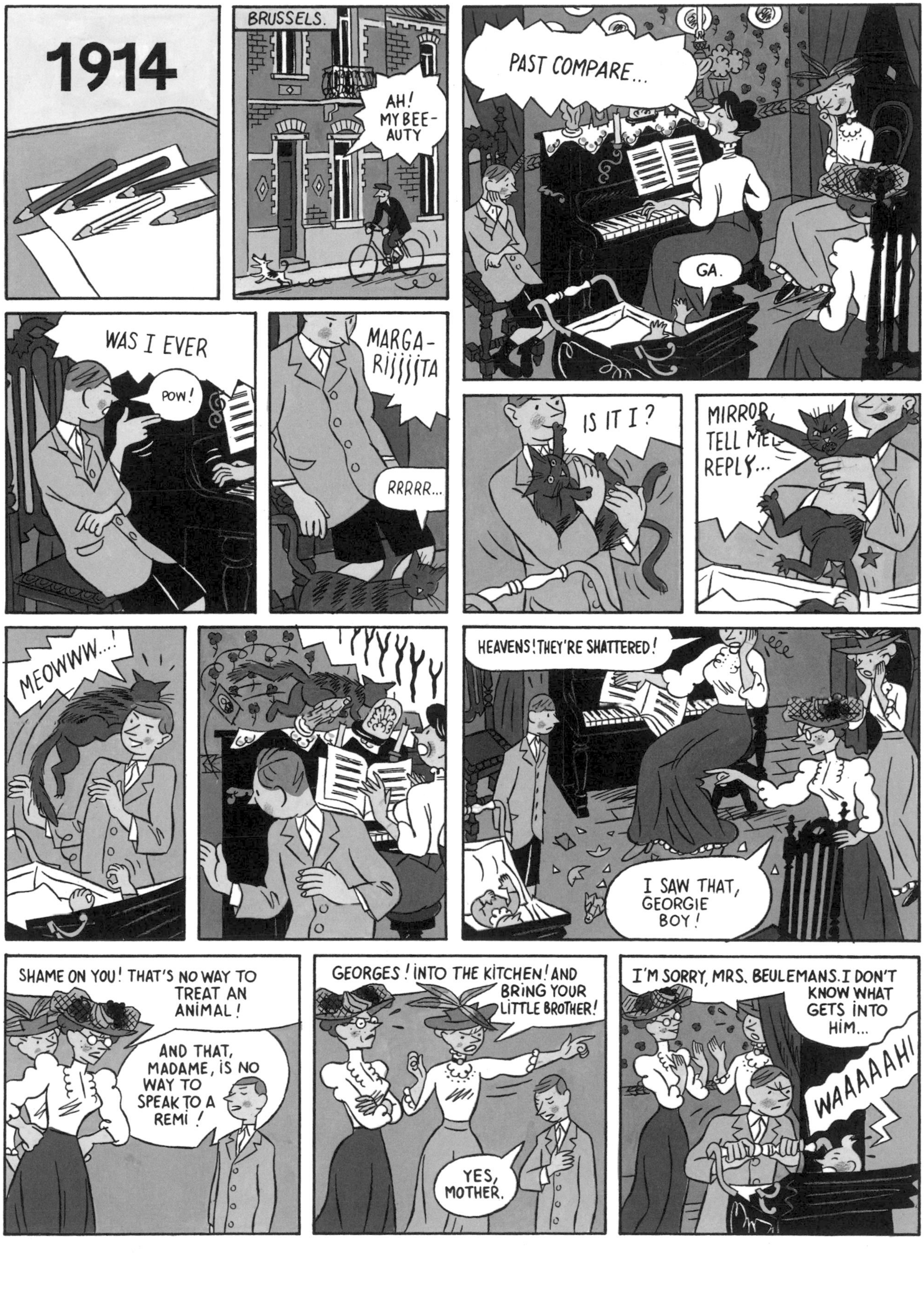
1914
BRUSSELS.
AH! MY BEE-AUTY
PAST COMPARE...
GA.
WAS I EVER
POW!
MARGA-RIiiiiiTA
RRRRR...
IS IT I?
MIRROR, TELL ME, REPLY...
MEOWWW...!
HEAVENS! THEY'RE SHATTERED!
I SAW THAT, GEORGIE BOY!
SHAME ON YOU! THAT'S NO WAY TO TREAT AN ANIMAL!
AND THAT, MADAME, IS NO WAY TO SPEAK TO A REMI!
GEORGES! INTO THE KITCHEN! AND BRING YOUR LITTLE BROTHER!
YES, MOTHER.
I'M SORRY, MRS. BEULEMANS. I DON'T KNOW WHAT GETS INTO HIM...
WAAAAAH!

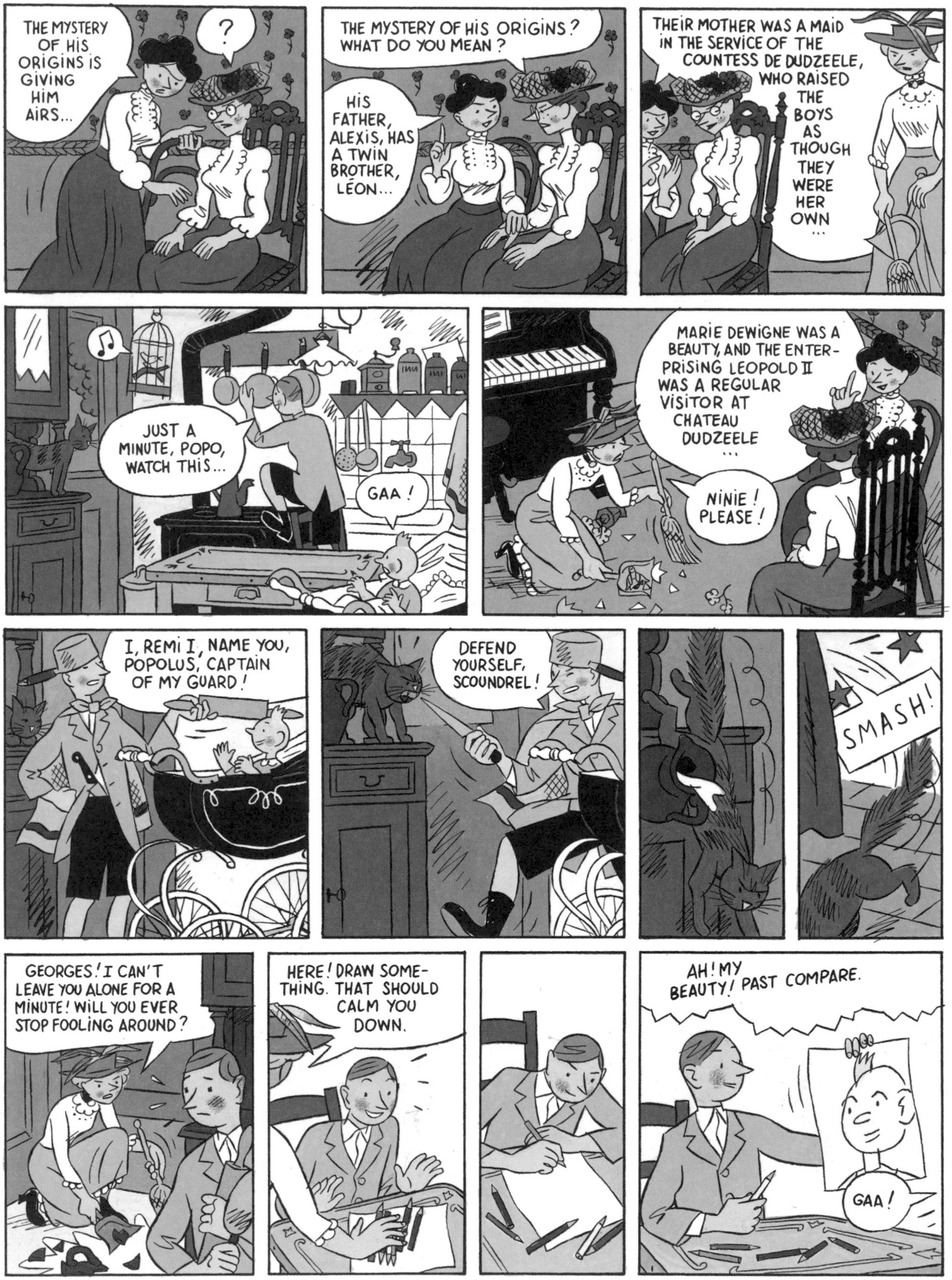

THE MYSTERY OF HIS ORIGINS IS GIVING HIM AIRS...
?
THE MYSTERY OF HIS ORIGINS? WHAT DO YOU MEAN?
HIS FATHER, ALEXIS, HAS A TWIN BROTHER, LÉON...
THEIR MOTHER WAS A MAID IN THE SERVICE OF THE COUNTESS DE DUDZEELE, WHO RAISED THE BOYS AS THOUGH THEY WERE HER OWN ...
JUST A MINUTE, POPO, WATCH THIS...
GAA!
MARIE DEWIGNE WAS A BEAUTY, AND THE ENTER-PRISING LEOPOLD II WAS A REGULAR VISITOR AT CHATEAU DUDZEELE ...
NINIE! PLEASE!
I, REMI I, NAME YOU, POPOLUS, CAPTAIN OF MY GUARD!
DEFEND YOURSELF, SCOUNDREL!
SMASH!
GEORGES! I CAN'T LEAVE YOU ALONE FOR A MINUTE! WILL YOU EVER STOP FOOLING AROUND?
HERE! DRAW SOME-THING. THAT SHOULD CALM YOU DOWN.
AH! MY BEAUTY! PAST COMPARE.
GAA!

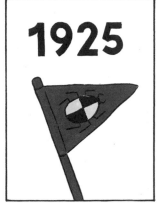

1925

GREAT ST. BERNARD PASS.

800 METERS FROM THE BORDER. WHAT A MESS.

I SEE THE PROBLEM, MY CHILDREN. JUST GIVE ME FIVE MINUTES!

TAKE HEART, BOYS! SCOUTS LAUGH IN THE FACE OF ADVERSITY!

BRUSSELS. ALEXIS, THE KHAKI CLOTH IS VERY ELEGANT. BELIEVE ME.

FOR CHILDREN?

SO, ARE THEY ON THEIR WAY?

YES, SIR.

YOU DON'T SEEM PLEASED ABOUT THIS PILGRIMAGE, REMI.

THAT'S NOT WHAT WORRIES ME, MR. VAN ROYE.

THROUGH RAIN AND MUD, ST. BONIFACE, YOUR VALIANT SCOUTS...

SO, CURIOUS FOX, ABANDONING YOUR TROOPS IN THE FACE OF ADVERSITY?

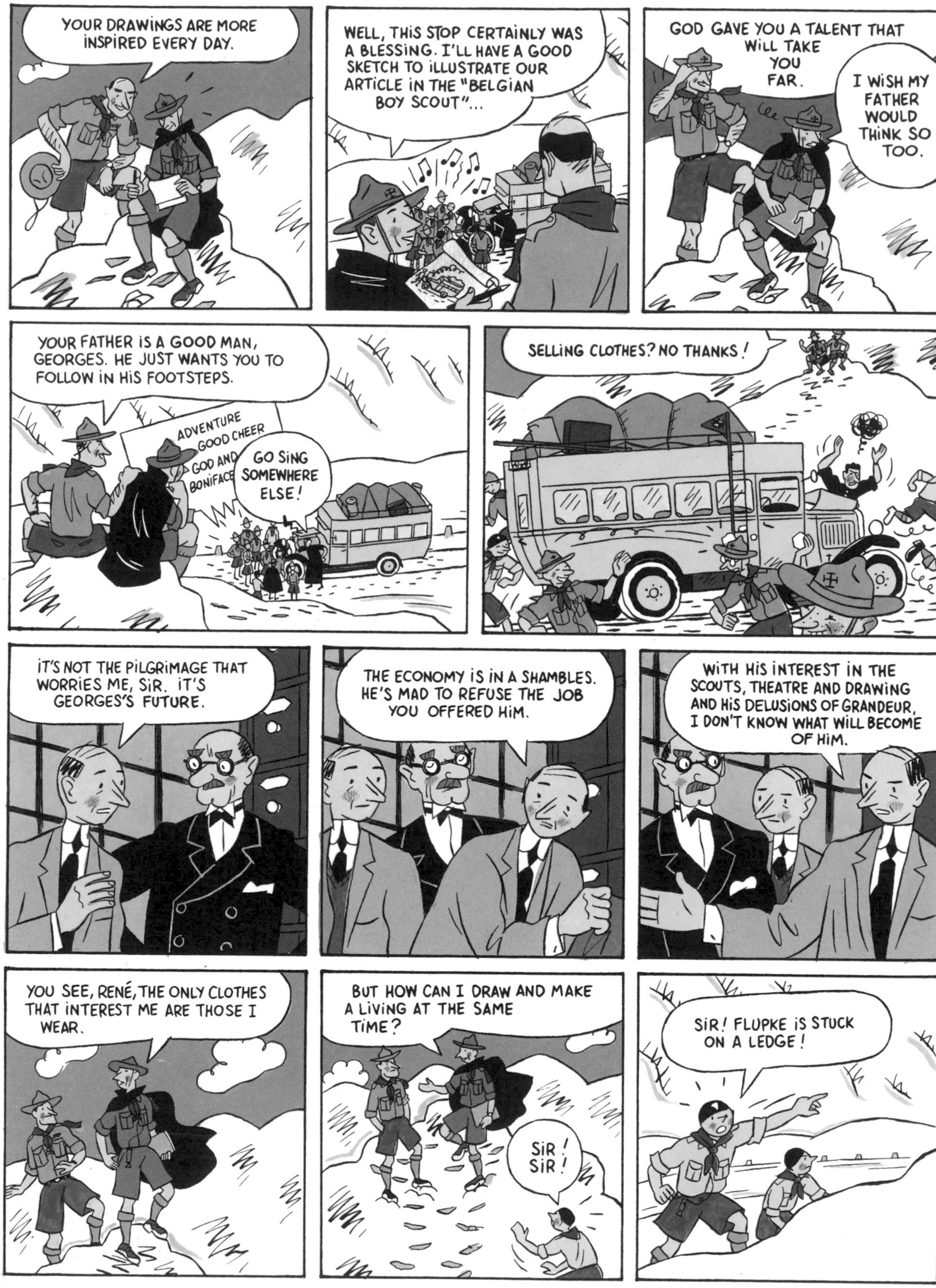
YOUR DRAWINGS ARE MORE INSPIRED EVERY DAY.
WELL, THIS STOP CERTAINLY WAS A BLESSING. I'LL HAVE A GOOD SKETCH TO ILLUSTRATE OUR ARTICLE IN THE "BELGIAN BOY SCOUT"...
GOD GAVE YOU A TALENT THAT WILL TAKE YOU FAR.
I WISH MY FATHER WOULD THINK SO TOO.
YOUR FATHER IS A GOOD MAN, GEORGES. HE JUST WANTS YOU TO FOLLOW IN HIS FOOTSTEPS.
ADVENTURE
GOOD CHEER
GOD AND BONIFACE
GO SING SOMEWHERE ELSE!
SELLING CLOTHES? NO THANKS!
IT'S NOT THE PILGRIMAGE THAT WORRIES ME, SIR. IT'S GEORGES'S FUTURE.
THE ECONOMY IS IN A SHAMBLES. HE'S MAD TO REFUSE THE JOB YOU OFFERED HIM.
WITH HIS INTEREST IN THE SCOUTS, THEATRE AND DRAWING AND HIS DELUSIONS OF GRANDEUR, I DON'T KNOW WHAT WILL BECOME OF HIM.
YOU SEE, RENÉ, THE ONLY CLOTHES THAT INTEREST ME ARE THOSE I WEAR.
BUT HOW CAN I DRAW AND MAKE A LIVING AT THE SAME TIME?
SIR! SIR!
SIR! FLUPKE IS STUCK ON A LEDGE!

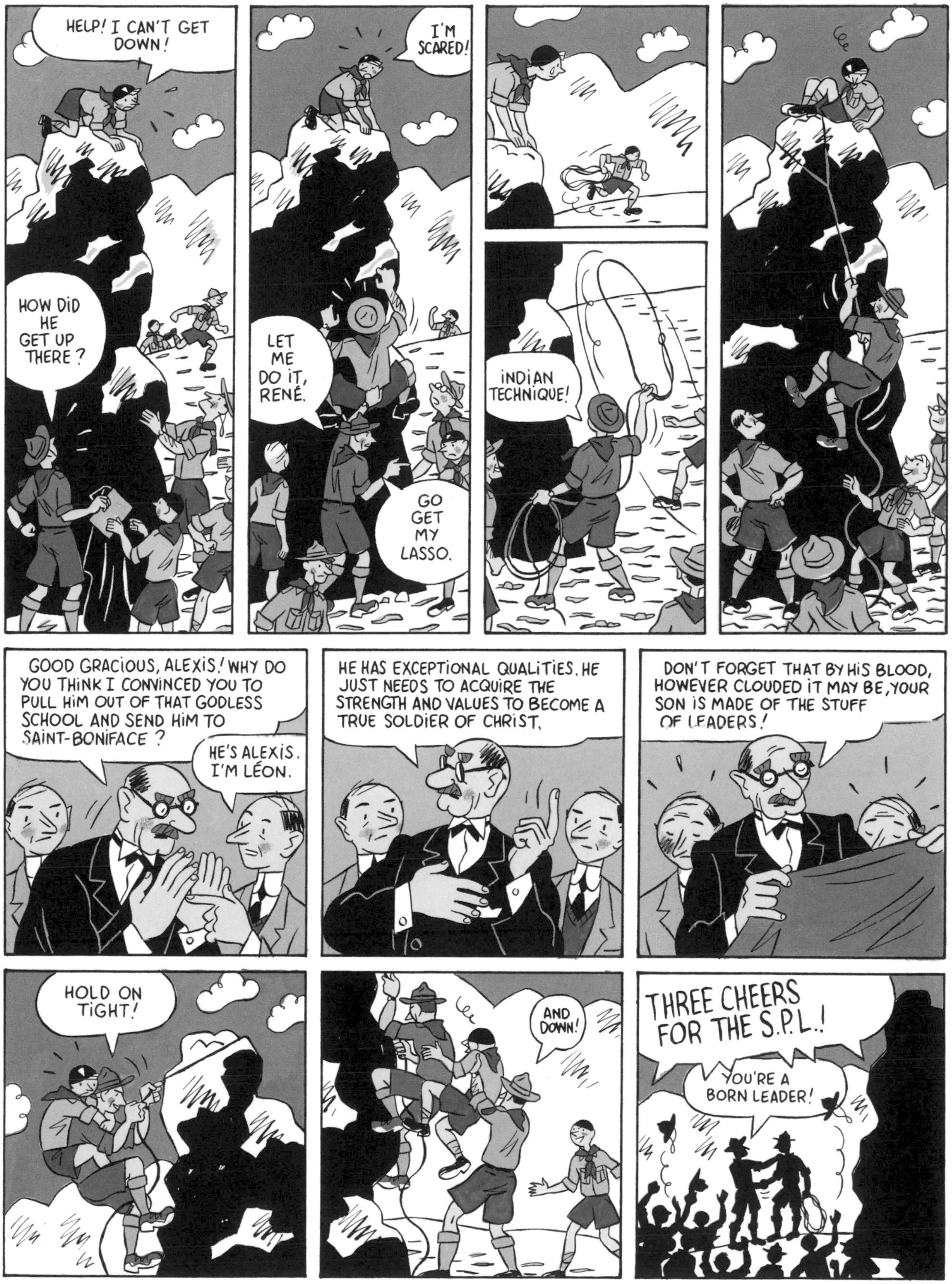
HELP! I CAN'T GET DOWN!
HOW DID HE GET UP THERE?
I'M SCARED!
LET ME DO IT, RENÉ.
GO GET MY LASSO.
INDIAN TECHNIQUE!
GOOD GRACIOUS, ALEXIS! WHY DO YOU THINK I CONVINCED YOU TO PULL HIM OUT OF THAT GODLESS SCHOOL AND SEND HIM TO SAINT-BONIFACE?
HE'S ALEXIS. I'M LÉON.
HE HAS EXCEPTIONAL QUALITIES. HE JUST NEEDS TO ACQUIRE THE STRENGTH AND VALUES TO BECOME A TRUE SOLDIER OF CHRIST.
DON'T FORGET THAT BY HIS BLOOD, HOWEVER CLOUDED IT MAY BE, YOUR SON IS MADE OF THE STUFF OF LEADERS!
HOLD ON TIGHT!
AND DOWN!
THREE CHEERS FOR THE S.P.L.!
YOU'RE A BORN LEADER!

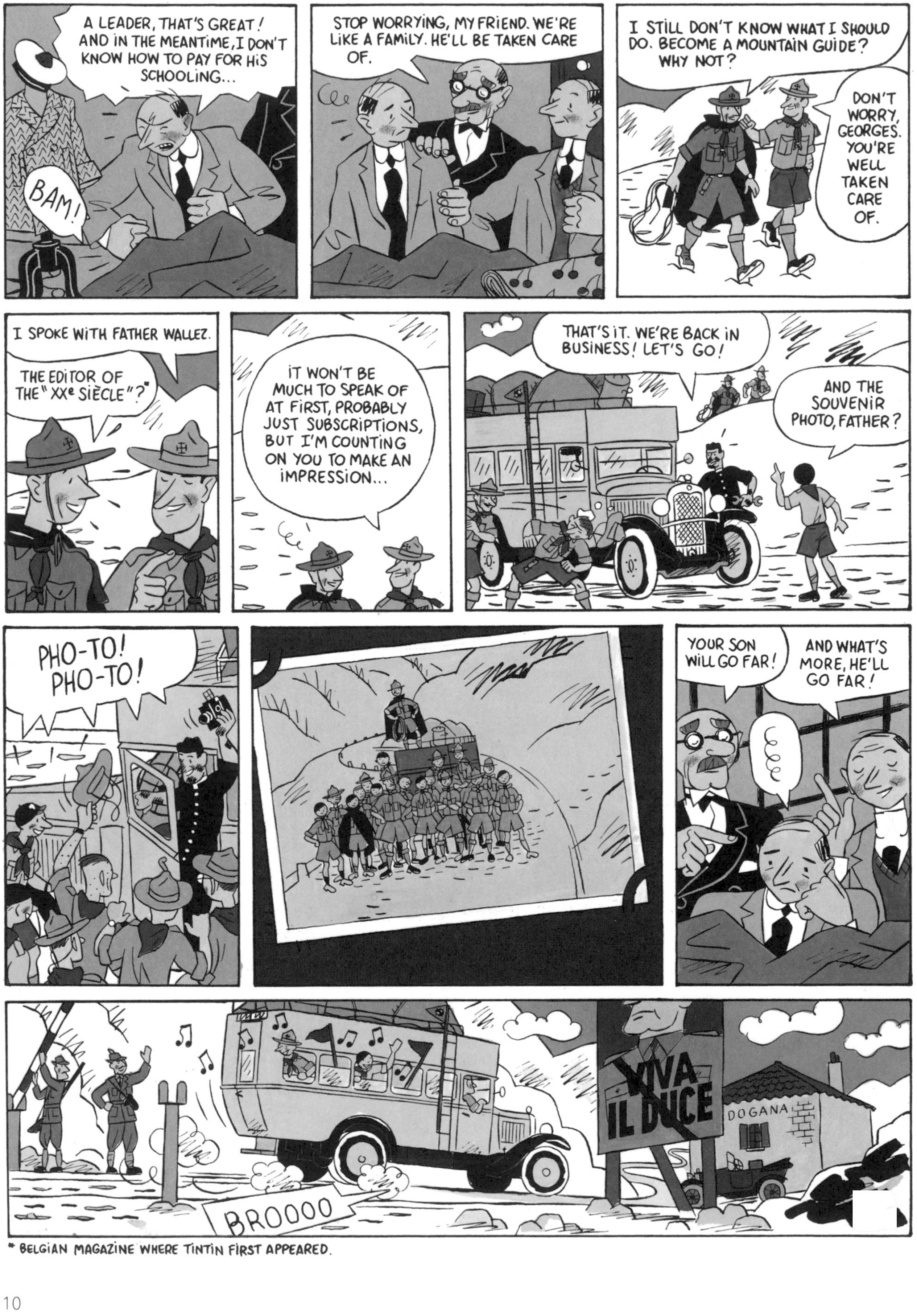
A LEADER, THAT'S GREAT! AND IN THE MEANTIME, I DON'T KNOW HOW TO PAY FOR HIS SCHOOLING...
BAM!
STOP WORRYING, MY FRIEND. WE'RE LIKE A FAMILY. HE'LL BE TAKEN CARE OF.
I STILL DON'T KNOW WHAT I SHOULD DO. BECOME A MOUNTAIN GUIDE? WHY NOT?
DON'T WORRY, GEORGES. YOU'RE WELL TAKEN CARE OF.
I SPOKE WITH FATHER WALLEZ.
THE EDITOR OF THE "XXe SIÈCLE"?*
IT WON'T BE MUCH TO SPEAK OF AT FIRST, PROBABLY JUST SUBSCRIPTIONS, BUT I'M COUNTING ON YOU TO MAKE AN IMPRESSION...
THAT'S IT. WE'RE BACK IN BUSINESS! LET'S GO!
AND THE SOUVENIR PHOTO, FATHER?
PHO-TO! PHO-TO!
YOUR SON WILL GO FAR!
AND WHAT'S MORE, HE'LL GO FAR!
VIVA IL DUCE
DOGANA
BROOOO

* BELGIAN MAGAZINE WHERE TINTIN FIRST APPEARED.

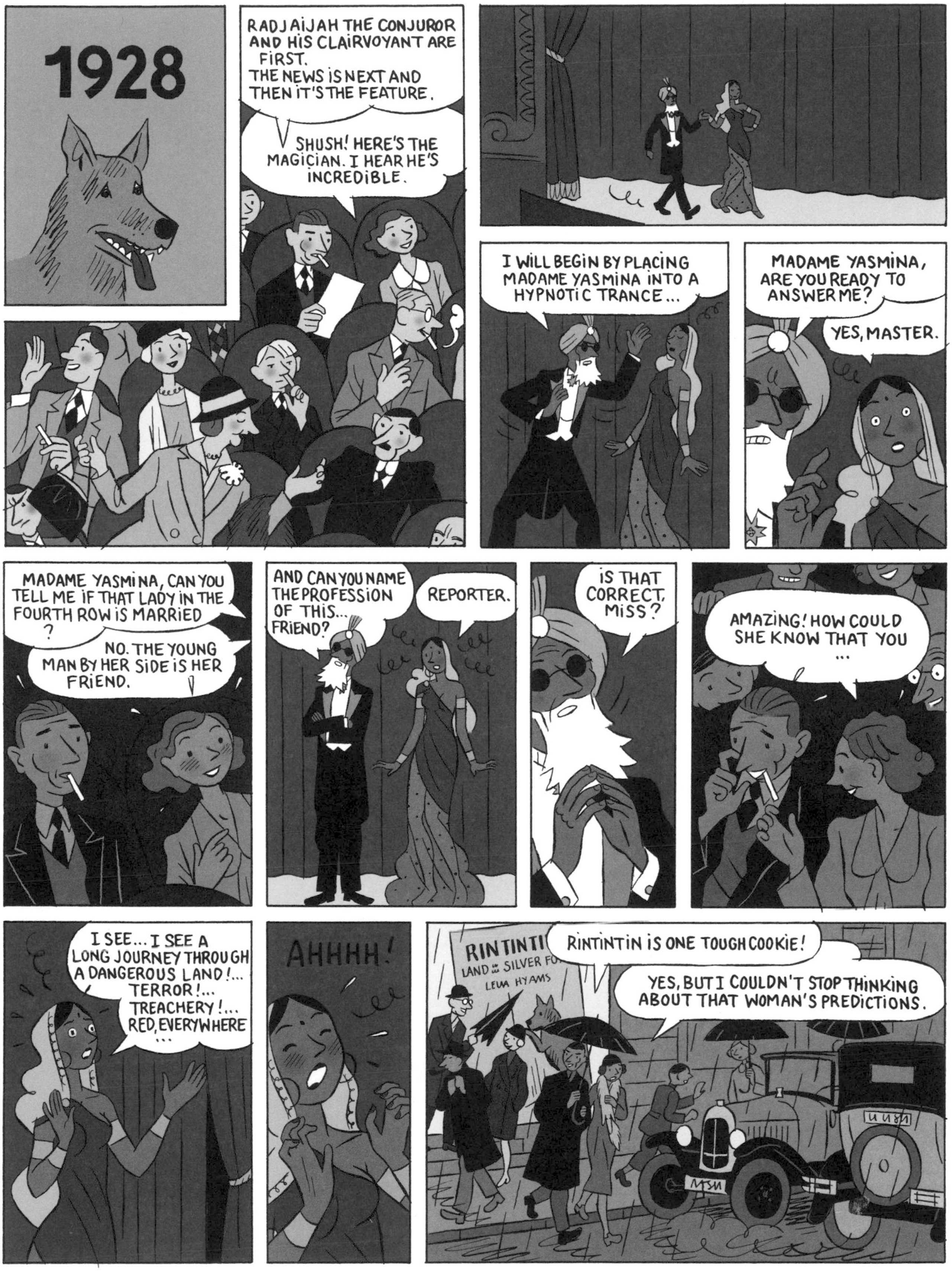
1928
RADJAIJAH THE CONJUROR AND HIS CLAIRVOYANT ARE FIRST. THE NEWS IS NEXT AND THEN IT'S THE FEATURE.
SHUSH! HERE'S THE MAGICIAN. I HEAR HE'S INCREDIBLE.
I WILL BEGIN BY PLACING MADAME YASMINA INTO A HYPNOTIC TRANCE...
MADAME YASMINA, ARE YOU READY TO ANSWER ME?
YES, MASTER.
MADAME YASMINA, CAN YOU TELL ME IF THAT LADY IN THE FOURTH ROW IS MARRIED?
NO. THE YOUNG MAN BY HER SIDE IS HER FRIEND.
AND CAN YOU NAME THE PROFESSION OF THIS... FRIEND?
REPORTER.
IS THAT CORRECT, MISS?
AMAZING! HOW COULD SHE KNOW THAT YOU ...
I SEE... I SEE A LONG JOURNEY THROUGH A DANGEROUS LAND!... TERROR!... TREACHERY!... RED, EVERYWHERE...
AHHHH!
RINTINTI
LAND OF THE SILVER FO
LEILA HYAMS
RINTINTIN IS ONE TOUGH COOKIE!
YES, BUT I COULDN'T STOP THINKING ABOUT THAT WOMAN'S PREDICTIONS.

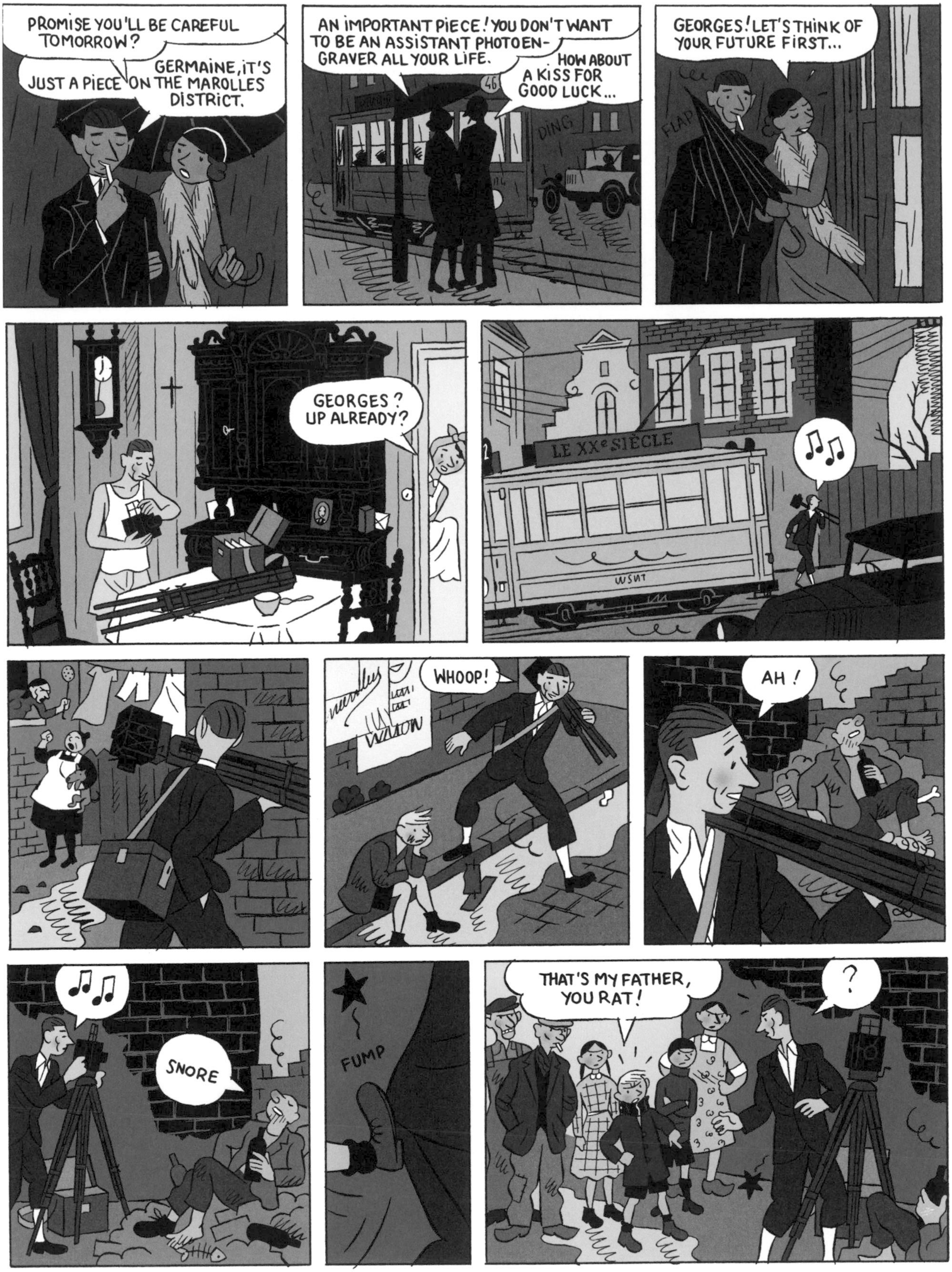
PROMISE YOU'LL BE CAREFUL TOMORROW?
GERMAINE, IT'S JUST A PIECE ON THE MAROLLES DISTRICT.
AN IMPORTANT PIECE! YOU DON'T WANT TO BE AN ASSISTANT PHOTOENGRAVER ALL YOUR LIFE.
HOW ABOUT A KISS FOR GOOD LUCK...
DING
GEORGES! LET'S THINK OF YOUR FUTURE FIRST...
FLAP
GEORGES? UP ALREADY?
LE XXe SIÈCLE
♫♫
WHOOP!
AH!
♫♫
SNORE
FUMP
THAT'S MY FATHER, YOU RAT!
?

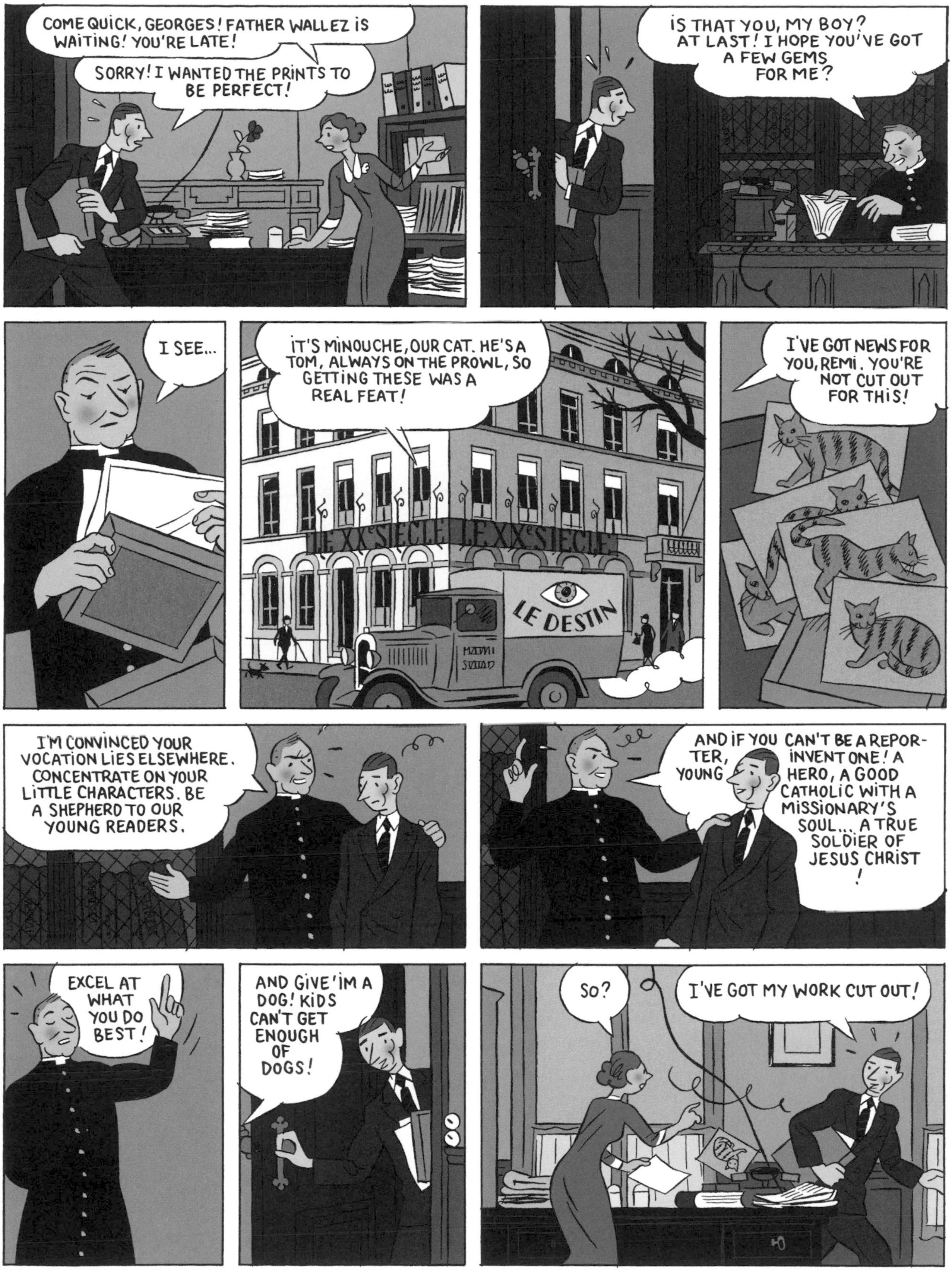
COME QUICK, GEORGES! FATHER WALLEZ IS WAITING! YOU'RE LATE!
SORRY! I WANTED THE PRINTS TO BE PERFECT!
IS THAT YOU, MY BOY? AT LAST! I HOPE YOU'VE GOT A FEW GEMS FOR ME?
I SEE...
IT'S MINOUCHE, OUR CAT. HE'S A TOM, ALWAYS ON THE PROWL, SO GETTING THESE WAS A REAL FEAT!
LE XXe SIÈCLE LE XXe SIÈCLE
LE DESTIN
I'VE GOT NEWS FOR YOU, REMI. YOU'RE NOT CUT OUT FOR THIS!
I'M CONVINCED YOUR VOCATION LIES ELSEWHERE. CONCENTRATE ON YOUR LITTLE CHARACTERS. BE A SHEPHERD TO OUR YOUNG READERS.
AND IF YOU CAN'T BE A REPORTER, YOUNG INVENT ONE! A HERO, A GOOD CATHOLIC WITH A MISSIONARY'S SOUL... A TRUE SOLDIER OF JESUS CHRIST!
EXCEL AT WHAT YOU DO BEST!
AND GIVE 'IM A DOG! KIDS CAN'T GET ENOUGH OF DOGS!
SO?
I'VE GOT MY WORK CUT OUT!

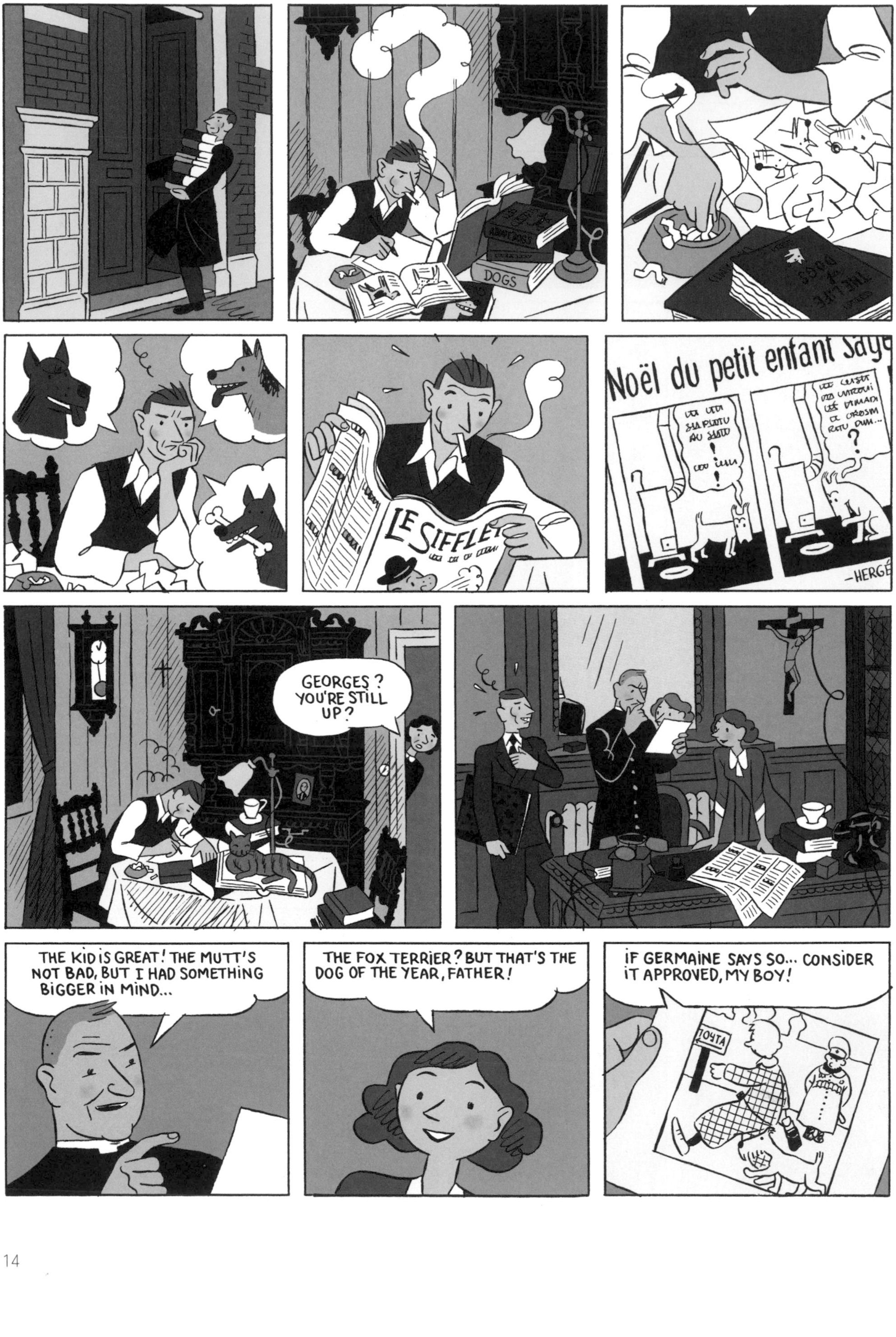
DOGS
Noël du petit enfant sage
LE SIFFLET
-HERGÉ
GEORGES? YOU'RE STILL UP?
THE KID IS GREAT! THE MUTT'S NOT BAD, BUT I HAD SOMETHING BIGGER IN MIND...
THE FOX TERRIER? BUT THAT'S THE DOG OF THE YEAR, FATHER!
IF GERMAINE SAYS SO... CONSIDER IT APPROVED, MY BOY!

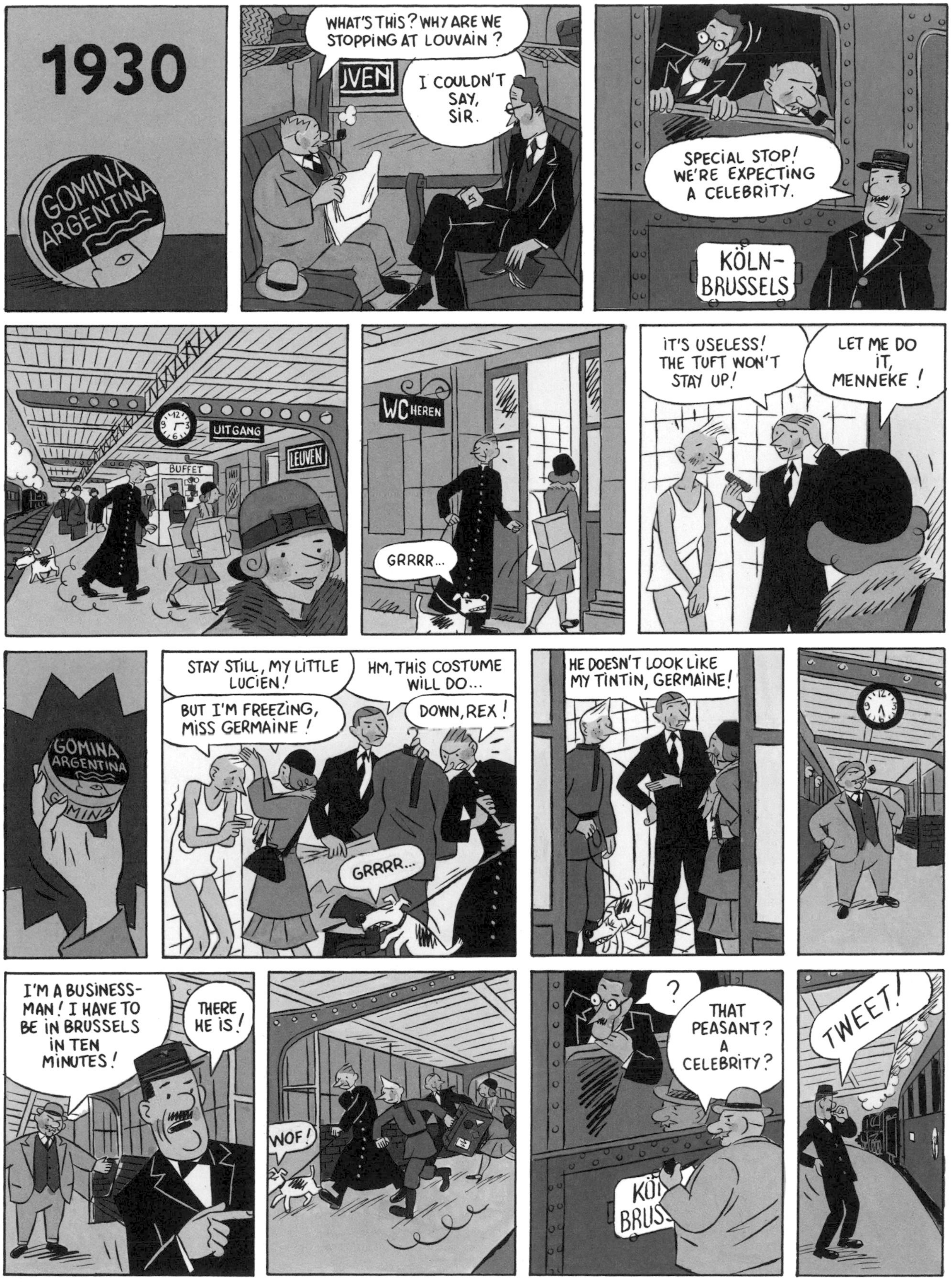
1930
GOMINA ARGENTINA
WHAT'S THIS? WHY ARE WE STOPPING AT LOUVAIN?
JVEN
I COULDN'T SAY, SIR.
SPECIAL STOP! WE'RE EXPECTING A CELEBRITY.
KÖLN-BRUSSELS
UITGANG
BUFFET
LEUVEN
WC HEREN
GRRRR...
IT'S USELESS! THE TUFT WON'T STAY UP!
LET ME DO IT, MENNEKE!
GOMINA ARGENTINA
STAY STILL, MY LITTLE LUCIEN!
BUT I'M FREEZING, MISS GERMAINE!
HM, THIS COSTUME WILL DO...
DOWN, REX!
GRRRR...
HE DOESN'T LOOK LIKE MY TINTIN, GERMAINE!
I'M A BUSINESSMAN! I HAVE TO BE IN BRUSSELS IN TEN MINUTES!
THERE HE IS!
WOF!
?
THAT PEASANT? A CELEBRITY?
TWEET!

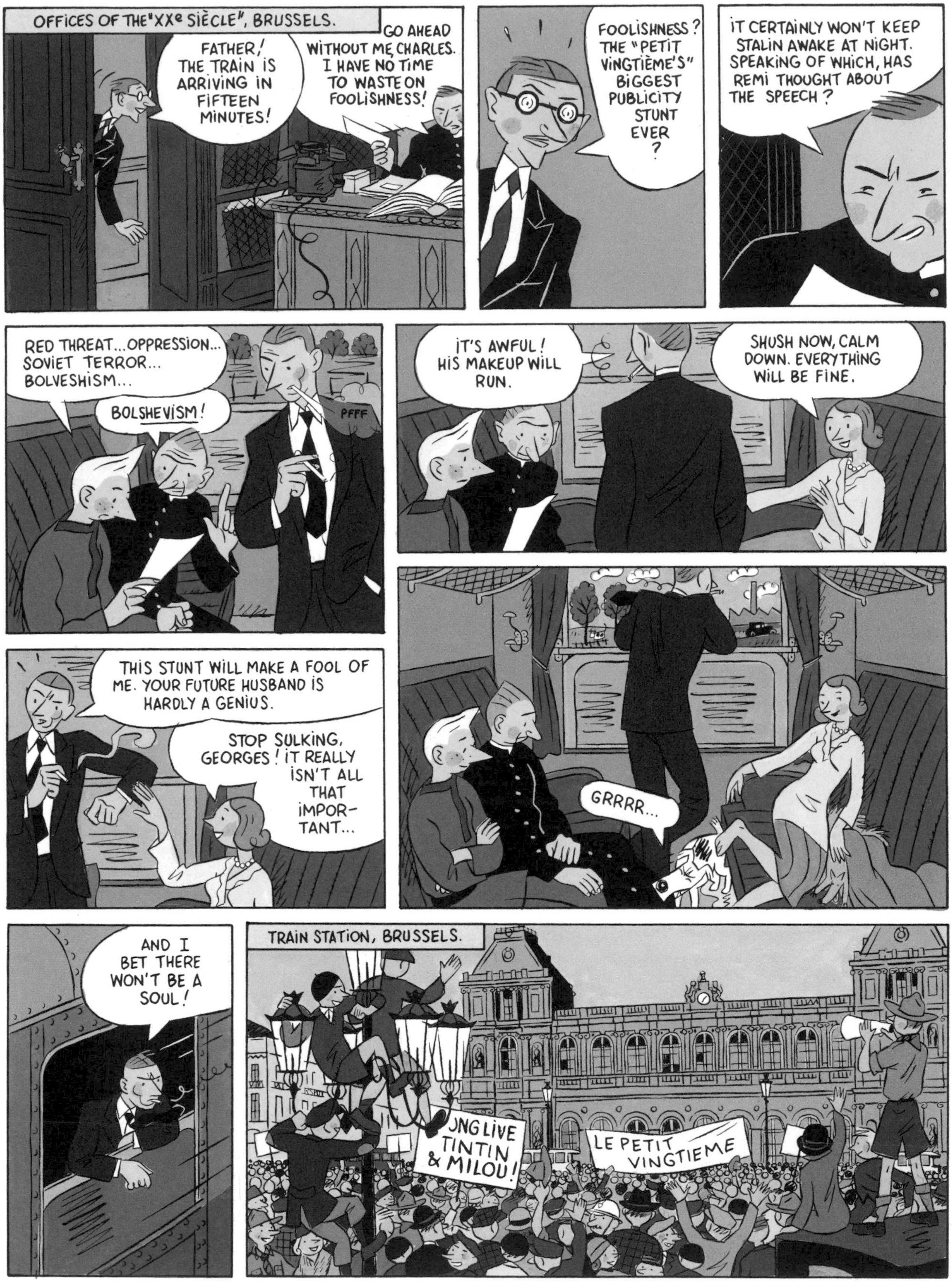
OFFICES OF THE "XXe SIÈCLE", BRUSSELS.
FATHER! THE TRAIN IS ARRIVING IN FIFTEEN MINUTES!
GO AHEAD WITHOUT ME, CHARLES. I HAVE NO TIME TO WASTE ON FOOLISHNESS!
FOOLISHNESS? THE "PETIT VINGTIÈME'S" BIGGEST PUBLICITY STUNT EVER?
IT CERTAINLY WON'T KEEP STALIN AWAKE AT NIGHT. SPEAKING OF WHICH, HAS REMI THOUGHT ABOUT THE SPEECH?
RED THREAT... OPPRESSION... SOVIET TERROR... BOLVESHISM...
BOLSHEVISM!
PFFF
IT'S AWFUL! HIS MAKEUP WILL RUN.
SHUSH NOW, CALM DOWN. EVERYTHING WILL BE FINE.
THIS STUNT WILL MAKE A FOOL OF ME. YOUR FUTURE HUSBAND IS HARDLY A GENIUS.
STOP SULKING, GEORGES! IT REALLY ISN'T ALL THAT IMPOR-TANT...
GRRRR...
AND I BET THERE WON'T BE A SOUL!
TRAIN STATION, BRUSSELS.
NG LIVE TINTIN & MILOU!
LE PETIT VINGTIEME

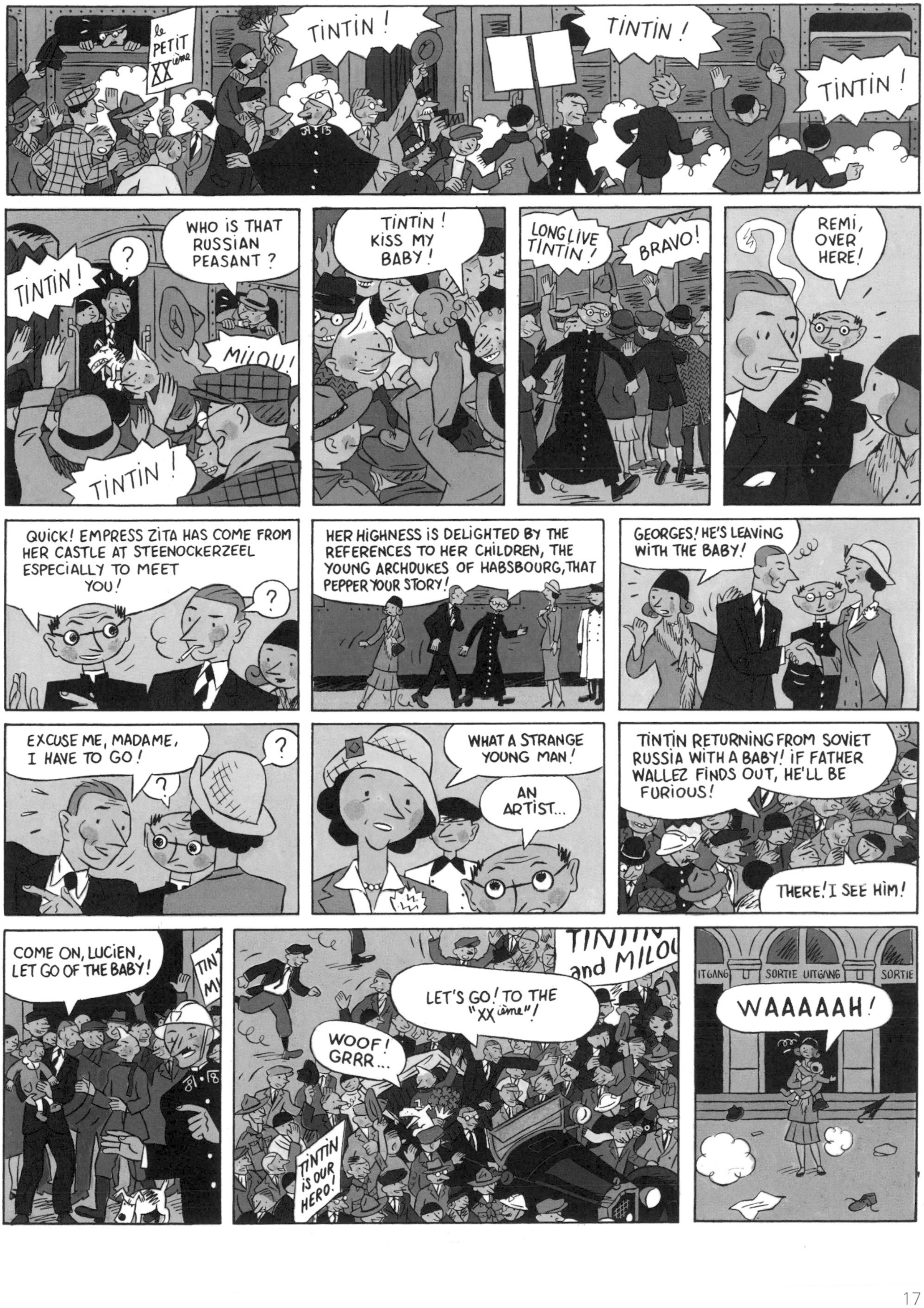
le PETIT XXième
TINTIN!
TINTIN!
TINTIN!
WHO IS THAT RUSSIAN PEASANT?
?
TINTIN!
MILOU!
TINTIN!
TINTIN! KISS MY BABY!
LONG LIVE TINTIN!
BRAVO!
REMI, OVER HERE!
QUICK! EMPRESS ZITA HAS COME FROM HER CASTLE AT STEENOCKERZEEL ESPECIALLY TO MEET YOU!
?
HER HIGHNESS IS DELIGHTED BY THE REFERENCES TO HER CHILDREN, THE YOUNG ARCHDUKES OF HABSBOURG, THAT PEPPER YOUR STORY!
GEORGES! HE'S LEAVING WITH THE BABY!
EXCUSE ME, MADAME, I HAVE TO GO!
?
?
WHAT A STRANGE YOUNG MAN!
AN ARTIST...
TINTIN RETURNING FROM SOVIET RUSSIA WITH A BABY! IF FATHER WALLEZ FINDS OUT, HE'LL BE FURIOUS!
THERE! I SEE HIM!
COME ON, LUCIEN, LET GO OF THE BABY!
and MILOU
LET'S GO! TO THE "XXième"!
WOOF! GRRR...
TINTIN IS OUR HERO!
UITGANG SORTIE UITGANG SORTIE
WAAAAAH!

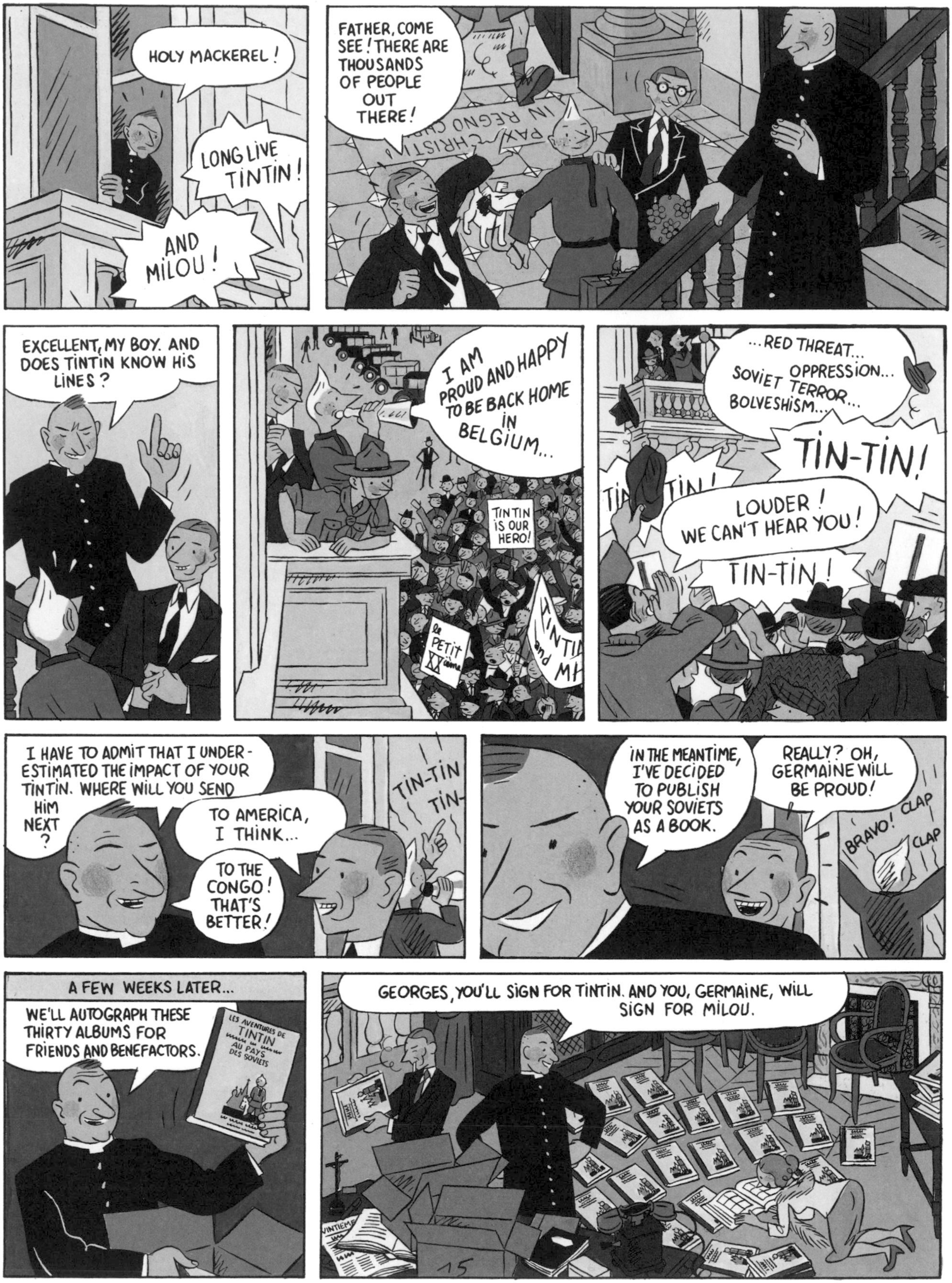
HOLY MACKEREL!
LONG LIVE TINTIN!
AND MILOU!
FATHER, COME SEE! THERE ARE THOUSANDS OF PEOPLE OUT THERE!
EXCELLENT, MY BOY. AND DOES TINTIN KNOW HIS LINES?
I AM PROUD AND HAPPY TO BE BACK HOME IN BELGIUM...
TINTIN IS OUR HERO!
...RED THREAT... OPPRESSION... SOVIET TERROR... BOLVESHISM...
TIN-TIN!
LOUDER! WE CAN'T HEAR YOU!
TIN-TIN!
I HAVE TO ADMIT THAT I UNDER-ESTIMATED THE IMPACT OF YOUR TINTIN. WHERE WILL YOU SEND HIM NEXT?
TO AMERICA, I THINK...
TO THE CONGO! THAT'S BETTER!
TIN-TIN TIN-
IN THE MEANTIME, I'VE DECIDED TO PUBLISH YOUR SOVIETS AS A BOOK.
REALLY? OH, GERMAINE WILL BE PROUD!
BRAVO! CLAP CLAP
A FEW WEEKS LATER...
WE'LL AUTOGRAPH THESE THIRTY ALBUMS FOR FRIENDS AND BENEFACTORS.
LES AVENTURES DE TINTIN AU PAYS DES SOVIETS
GEORGES, YOU'LL SIGN FOR TINTIN. AND YOU, GERMAINE, WILL SIGN FOR MILOU.

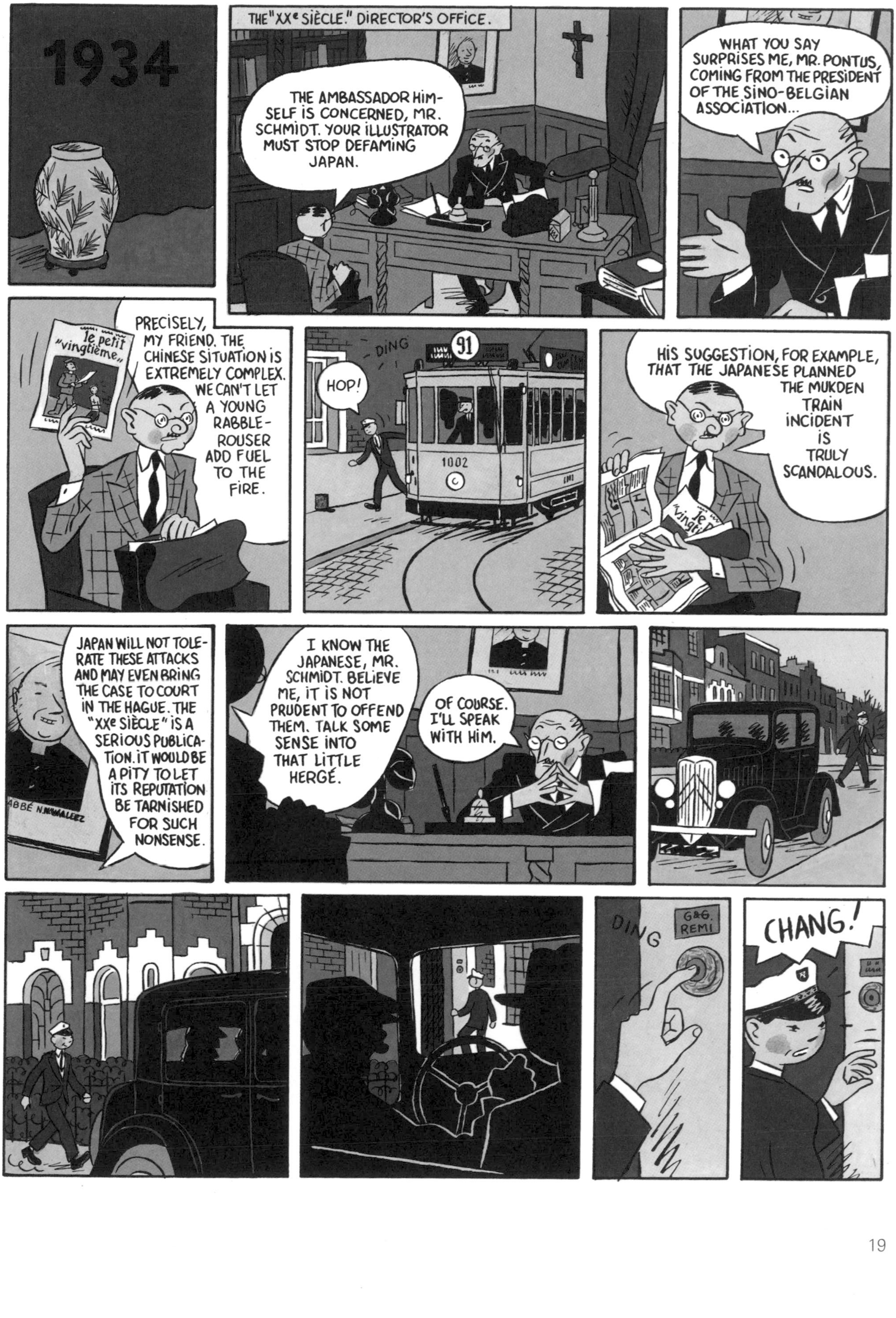
1934
THE "XXe SIÈCLE." DIRECTOR'S OFFICE.
THE AMBASSADOR HIMSELF IS CONCERNED, MR. SCHMIDT. YOUR ILLUSTRATOR MUST STOP DEFAMING JAPAN.
WHAT YOU SAY SURPRISES ME, MR. PONTUS, COMING FROM THE PRESIDENT OF THE SINO-BELGIAN ASSOCIATION...
le petit "vingtième"
PRECISELY, MY FRIEND. THE CHINESE SITUATION IS EXTREMELY COMPLEX. WE CAN'T LET A YOUNG RABBLE-ROUSER ADD FUEL TO THE FIRE.
DING
91
HOP!
1002
HIS SUGGESTION, FOR EXAMPLE, THAT THE JAPANESE PLANNED THE MUKDEN TRAIN INCIDENT IS TRULY SCANDALOUS.
JAPAN WILL NOT TOLERATE THESE ATTACKS AND MAY EVEN BRING THE CASE TO COURT IN THE HAGUE. THE "XXe SIÈCLE" IS A SERIOUS PUBLICATION. IT WOULD BE A PITY TO LET ITS REPUTATION BE TARNISHED FOR SUCH NONSENSE.
I KNOW THE JAPANESE, MR. SCHMIDT. BELIEVE ME, IT IS NOT PRUDENT TO OFFEND THEM. TALK SOME SENSE INTO THAT LITTLE HERGÉ.
OF COURSE. I'LL SPEAK WITH HIM.
DING
G&G. REMI
CHANG!

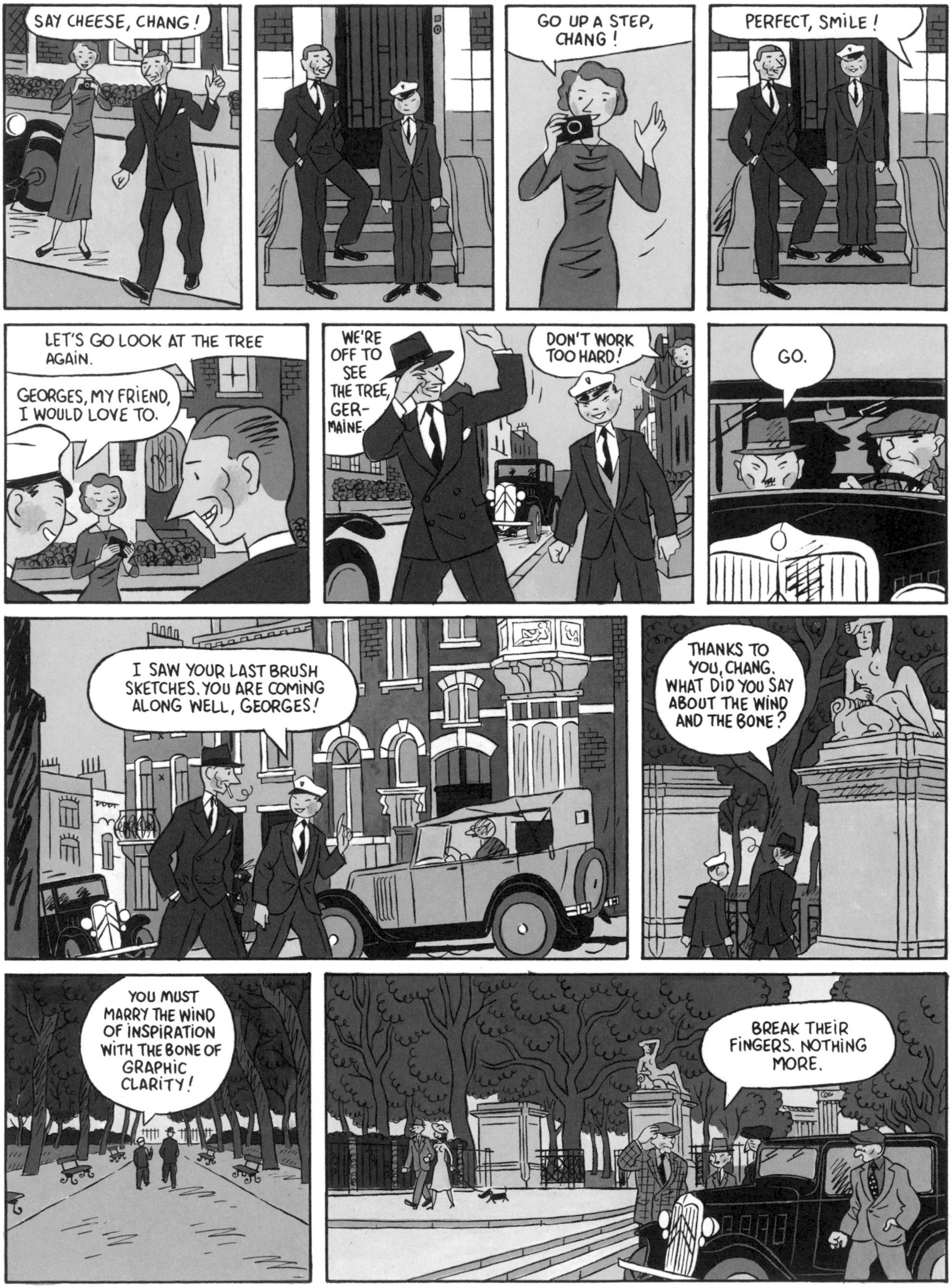
SAY CHEESE, CHANG!
GO UP A STEP, CHANG!
PERFECT, SMILE!
LET'S GO LOOK AT THE TREE AGAIN.
GEORGES, MY FRIEND, I WOULD LOVE TO.
WE'RE OFF TO SEE THE TREE, GERMAINE.
DON'T WORK TOO HARD!
GO.
I SAW YOUR LAST BRUSH SKETCHES. YOU ARE COMING ALONG WELL, GEORGES!
THANKS TO YOU, CHANG. WHAT DID YOU SAY ABOUT THE WIND AND THE BONE?
YOU MUST MARRY THE WIND OF INSPIRATION WITH THE BONE OF GRAPHIC CLARITY!
BREAK THEIR FINGERS. NOTHING MORE.

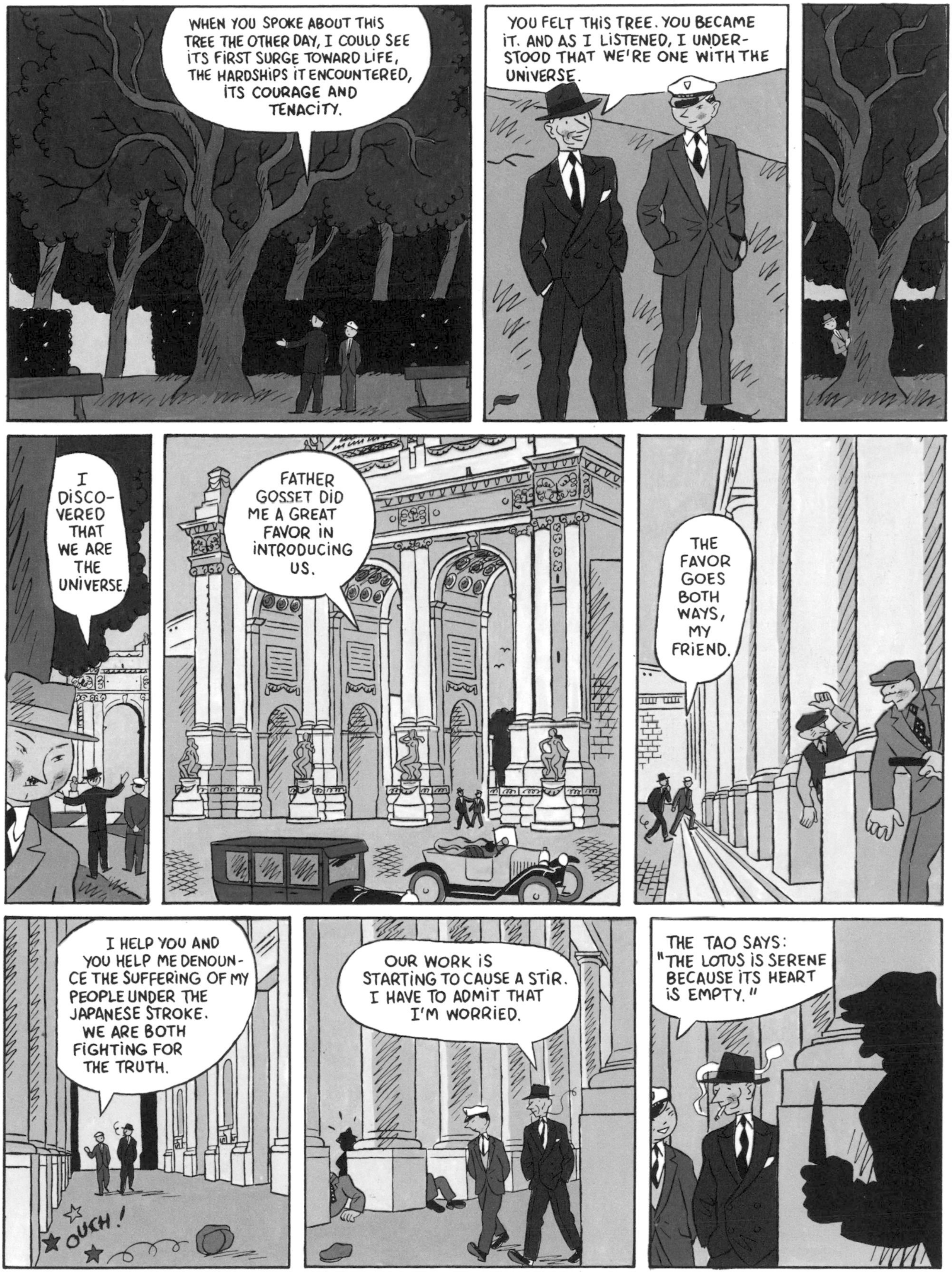
WHEN YOU SPOKE ABOUT THIS TREE THE OTHER DAY, I COULD SEE ITS FIRST SURGE TOWARD LIFE, THE HARDSHIPS IT ENCOUNTERED, ITS COURAGE AND TENACITY.
YOU FELT THIS TREE. YOU BECAME IT. AND AS I LISTENED, I UNDERSTOOD THAT WE'RE ONE WITH THE UNIVERSE.
I DISCOVERED THAT WE ARE THE UNIVERSE.
FATHER GOSSET DID ME A GREAT FAVOR IN INTRODUCING US.
THE FAVOR GOES BOTH WAYS, MY FRIEND.
I HELP YOU AND YOU HELP ME DENOUNCE THE SUFFERING OF MY PEOPLE UNDER THE JAPANESE STROKE. WE ARE BOTH FIGHTING FOR THE TRUTH.
OUCH!
OUR WORK IS STARTING TO CAUSE A STIR. I HAVE TO ADMIT THAT I'M WORRIED.
THE TAO SAYS: "THE LOTUS IS SERENE BECAUSE ITS HEART IS EMPTY."

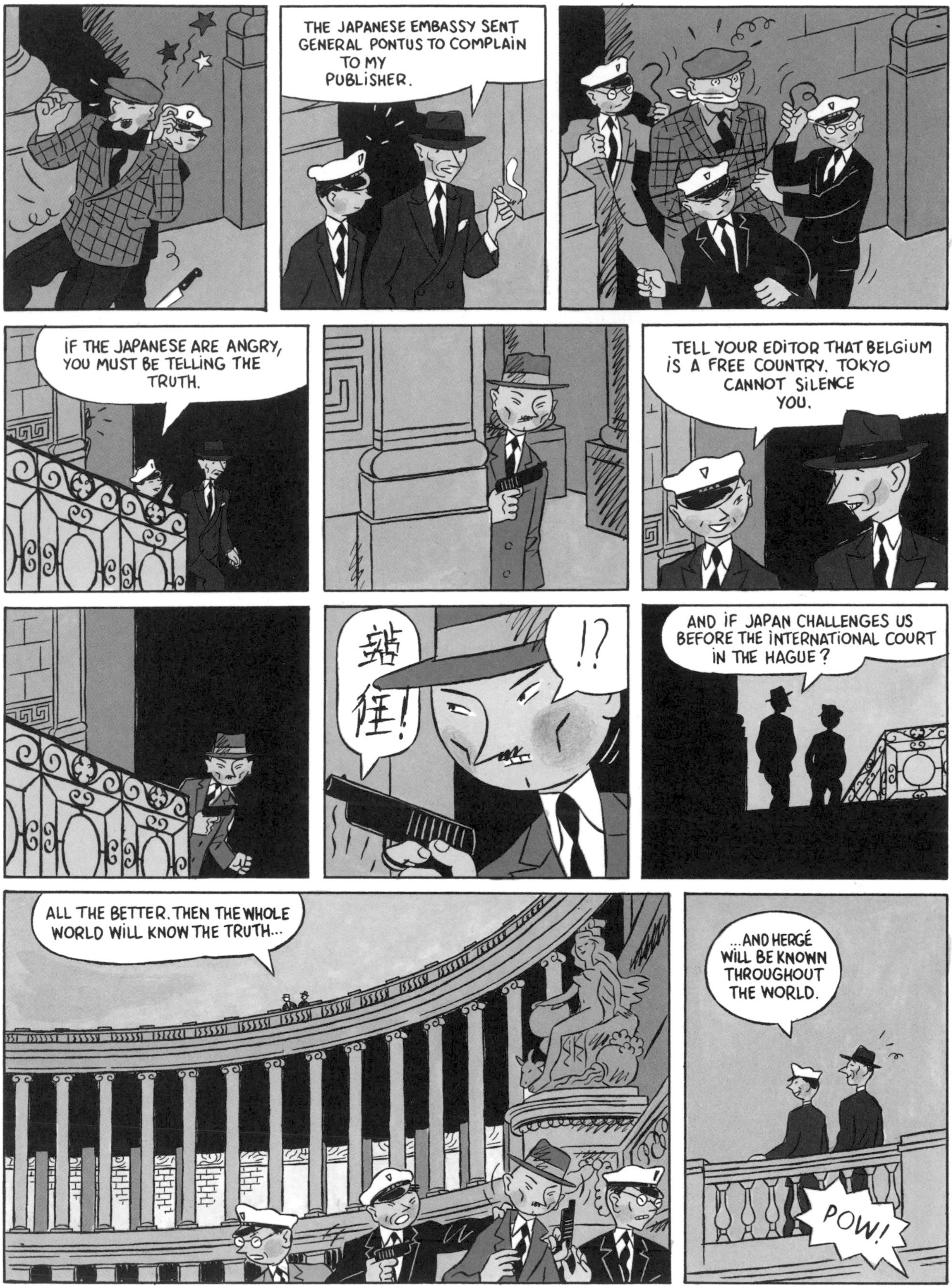
THE JAPANESE EMBASSY SENT GENERAL PONTUS TO COMPLAIN TO MY PUBLISHER.
IF THE JAPANESE ARE ANGRY, YOU MUST BE TELLING THE TRUTH.
TELL YOUR EDITOR THAT BELGIUM IS A FREE COUNTRY. TOKYO CANNOT SILENCE YOU.
站住!
!?
AND IF JAPAN CHALLENGES US BEFORE THE INTERNATIONAL COURT IN THE HAGUE?
ALL THE BETTER. THEN THE WHOLE WORLD WILL KNOW THE TRUTH...
...AND HERGÉ WILL BE KNOWN THROUGHOUT THE WORLD.
POW!

1941

GALERIES SAINT-HUBERT, BRUSSELS.

CLANG! CLANG! CLANG! CLANG!

NO, NO, TOO LATE. THE SHOW HAS BEGUN!

THEATRE ROYAL DES GALERIES

TINTIN IN INDIA
or
THE MYSTERY
OF THE
BLUE DIAMOND

A PLAY IN THREE ACT
BY
HERGÉ &
J. VAN MELKEBEKE
DIRECTED BY

CLANG! CLANG! CLANG! CLANG!

LET'S GO, DARLINGS. ON STAGE!

VAN MELK, THE MAHARAJA'S SPEECH SEEMS A BIT WEAK.

TRUE! IT ISN'T KING LEAR...

BUT IT'S NOT BAD FOR A PIECE OF JUNK THAT WAS COBBLED TO-GETHER IN A FEW WEEKS.

JUNK?

PLEASE ACCEPT THE TITLE OF CHIEF COUNSELOR TO THE MAHARAJA.

ALL RIGHT, AGREED. I'LL STAY.

TING

TING

TING

?

MR. VAN MELKEBEKE?

22

AH, THERE'S OUR FRIEND!

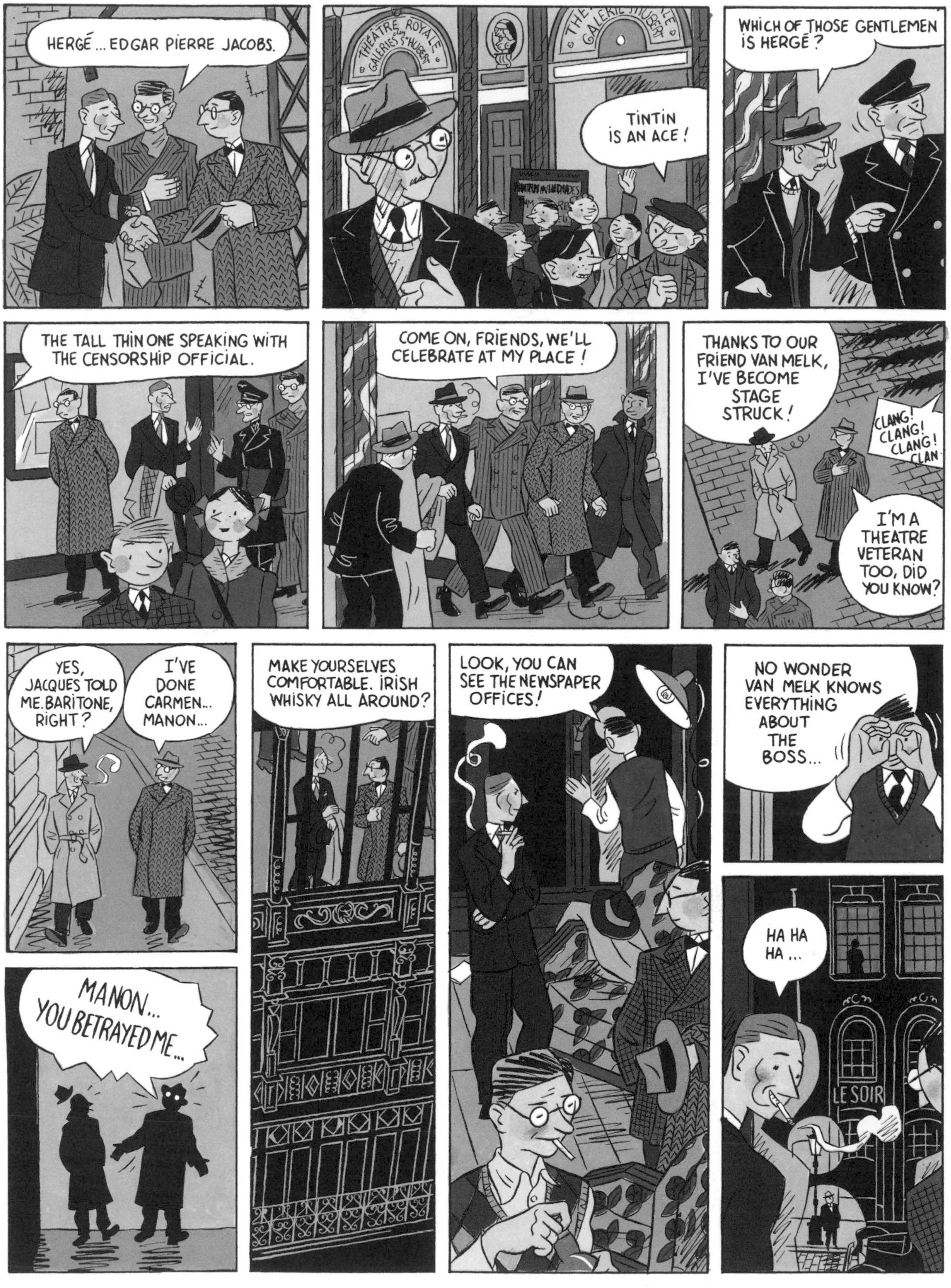

HERGÉ... EDGAR PIERRE JACOBS.
THEATRE ROYALE GALERIES ST-HUBERT
TINTIN IS AN ACE!
WHICH OF THOSE GENTLEMEN IS HERGÉ?
THE TALL THIN ONE SPEAKING WITH THE CENSORSHIP OFFICIAL.
COME ON, FRIENDS, WE'LL CELEBRATE AT MY PLACE!
THANKS TO OUR FRIEND VAN MELK, I'VE BECOME STAGE STRUCK!
CLANG! CLANG! CLANG! CLAN
I'M A THEATRE VETERAN TOO, DID YOU KNOW?
YES, JACQUES TOLD ME. BARITONE, RIGHT?
I'VE DONE CARMEN... MANON...
MANON... YOU BETRAYED ME...
MAKE YOURSELVES COMFORTABLE. IRISH WHISKY ALL AROUND?
LOOK, YOU CAN SEE THE NEWSPAPER OFFICES!
NO WONDER VAN MELK KNOWS EVERYTHING ABOUT THE BOSS...
HA HA HA...
LE SOIR

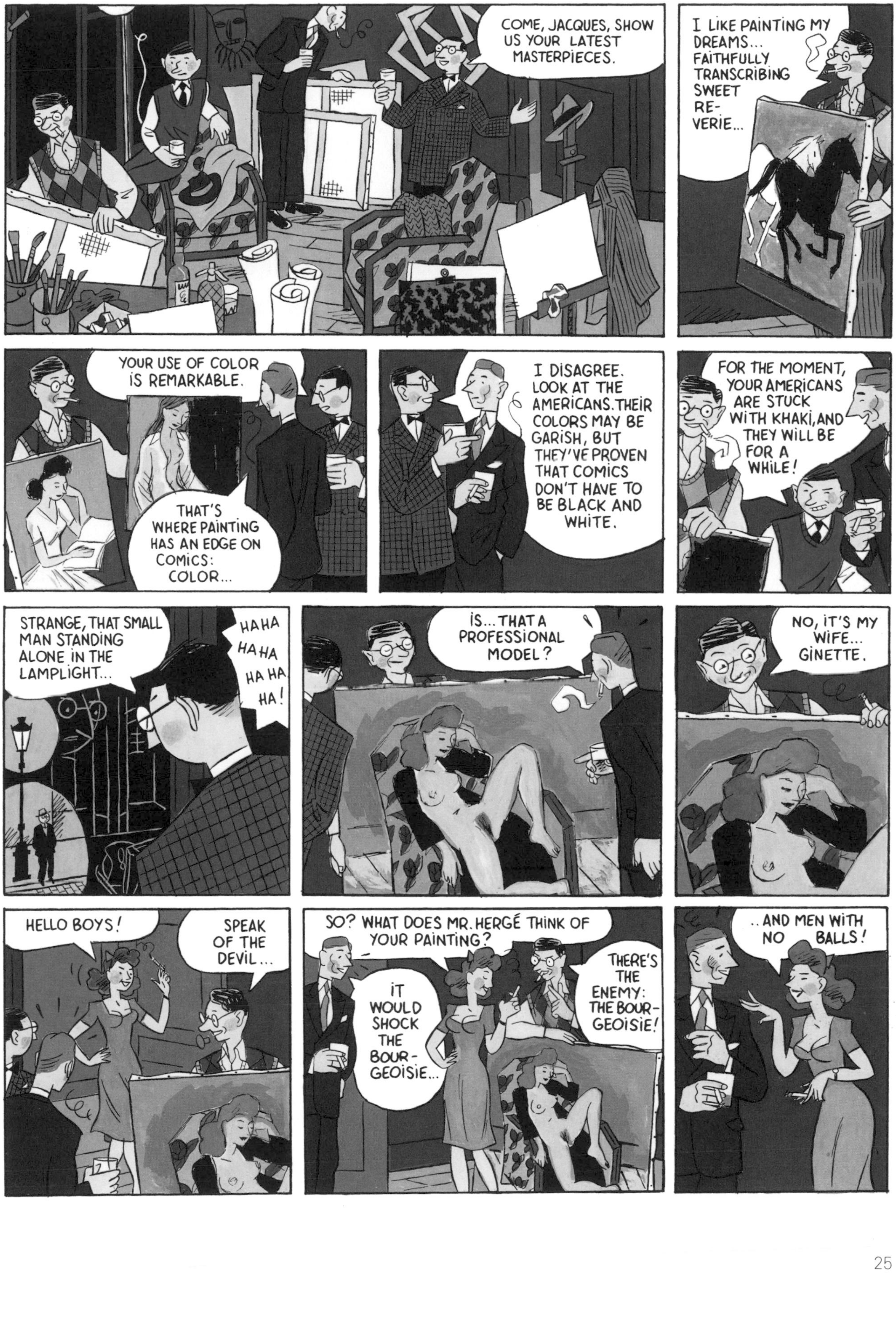
COME, JACQUES, SHOW US YOUR LATEST MASTERPIECES.
I LIKE PAINTING MY DREAMS... FAITHFULLY TRANSCRIBING SWEET RE-VERIE...
YOUR USE OF COLOR IS REMARKABLE.
THAT'S WHERE PAINTING HAS AN EDGE ON COMICS: COLOR...
I DISAGREE. LOOK AT THE AMERICANS. THEIR COLORS MAY BE GARISH, BUT THEY'VE PROVEN THAT COMICS DON'T HAVE TO BE BLACK AND WHITE.
FOR THE MOMENT, YOUR AMERICANS ARE STUCK WITH KHAKI, AND THEY WILL BE FOR A WHILE!
STRANGE, THAT SMALL MAN STANDING ALONE IN THE LAMPLIGHT...
HA HA HA HA HA HA HA!
IS... THAT A PROFESSIONAL MODEL?
NO, IT'S MY WIFE... GINETTE.
HELLO BOYS!
SPEAK OF THE DEVIL...
SO? WHAT DOES MR. HERGÉ THINK OF YOUR PAINTING?
IT WOULD SHOCK THE BOUR-GEOISIE...
THERE'S THE ENEMY: THE BOUR-GEOISIE!
.. AND MEN WITH NO BALLS!

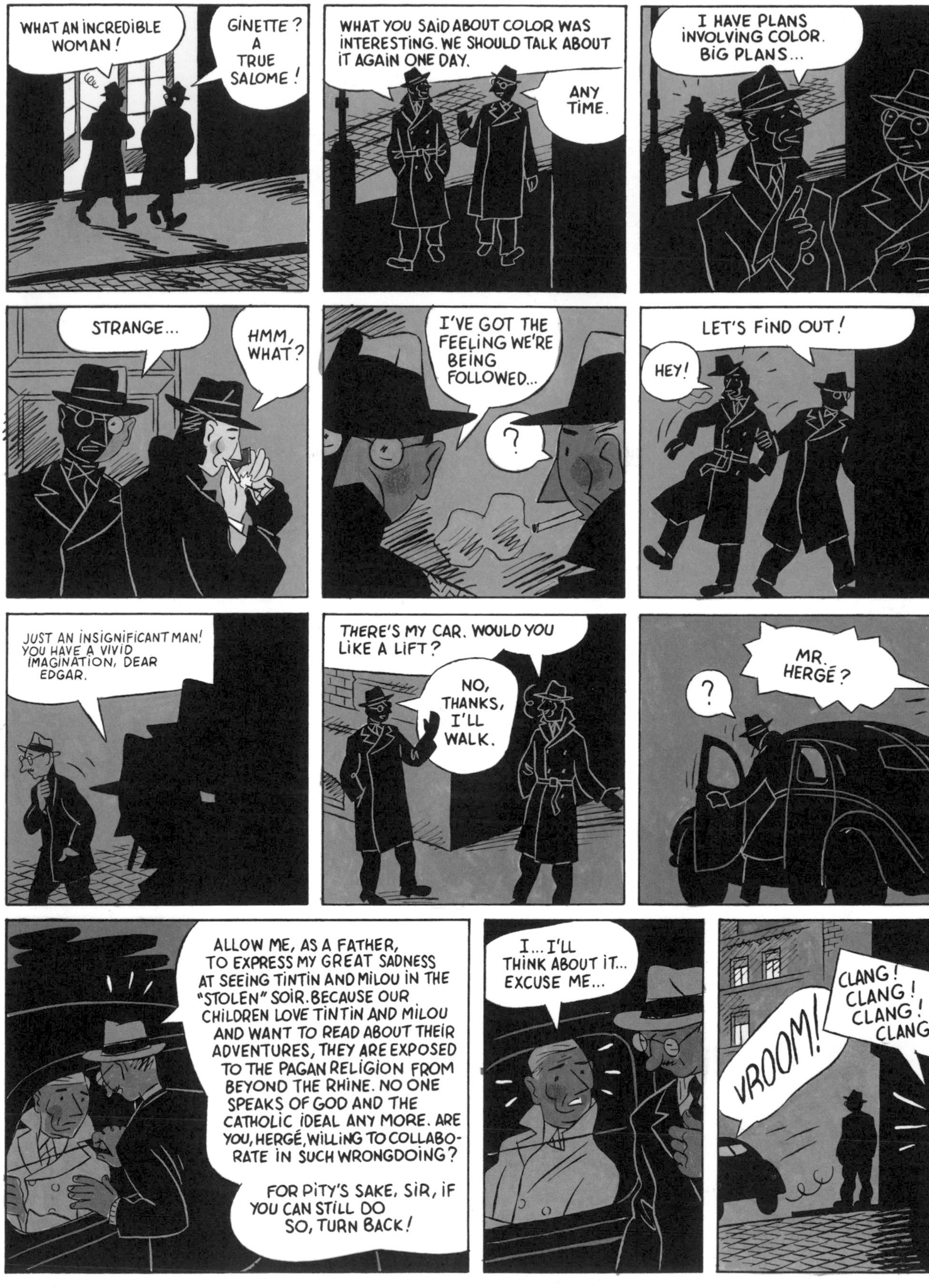
WHAT AN INCREDIBLE WOMAN!
GINETTE? A TRUE SALOME!
WHAT YOU SAID ABOUT COLOR WAS INTERESTING. WE SHOULD TALK ABOUT IT AGAIN ONE DAY.
ANY TIME.
I HAVE PLANS INVOLVING COLOR. BIG PLANS...
STRANGE...
HMM, WHAT?
I'VE GOT THE FEELING WE'RE BEING FOLLOWED...
?
LET'S FIND OUT!
HEY!
JUST AN INSIGNIFICANT MAN! YOU HAVE A VIVID IMAGINATION, DEAR EDGAR.
THERE'S MY CAR. WOULD YOU LIKE A LIFT?
NO, THANKS, I'LL WALK.
MR. HERGÉ?
?
ALLOW ME, AS A FATHER, TO EXPRESS MY GREAT SADNESS AT SEEING TINTIN AND MILOU IN THE "STOLEN" SOIR. BECAUSE OUR CHILDREN LOVE TINTIN AND MILOU AND WANT TO READ ABOUT THEIR ADVENTURES, THEY ARE EXPOSED TO THE PAGAN RELIGION FROM BEYOND THE RHINE. NO ONE SPEAKS OF GOD AND THE CATHOLIC IDEAL ANY MORE. ARE YOU, HERGÉ, WILLING TO COLLABORATE IN SUCH WRONGDOING?
FOR PITY'S SAKE, SIR, IF YOU CAN STILL DO SO, TURN BACK!
I... I'LL THINK ABOUT IT... EXCUSE ME...
VROOM!
CLANG! CLANG! CLANG! CLANG!

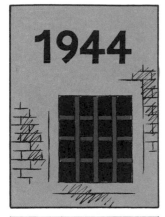

1944

BOISFORT. DECEMBER 1943.

YOU WERE RIGHT, EDGAR! THIS IS EXACTLY WHAT WE NEED!

YOU'RE SURE IT'S EMPTY?

I THINK SO...

VOILA! THE HOME OF PROFESSOR TARRAGON!

I THINK WE SHOULD GET GOING...

VROOOM

VROOOOM

THAT WAS CLOSE. I THINK WE JUST NARROWLY ESCAPED A FEW EMBARRASSING QUESTIONS!

BAH. EVERYBODY LOVES TINTIN!

SEPTEMBER 3, 1944. LIBERATION OF BRUSSELS.

SLIME!

TRAITOR!

BASTARD!

PROFITEER!

TOOT!

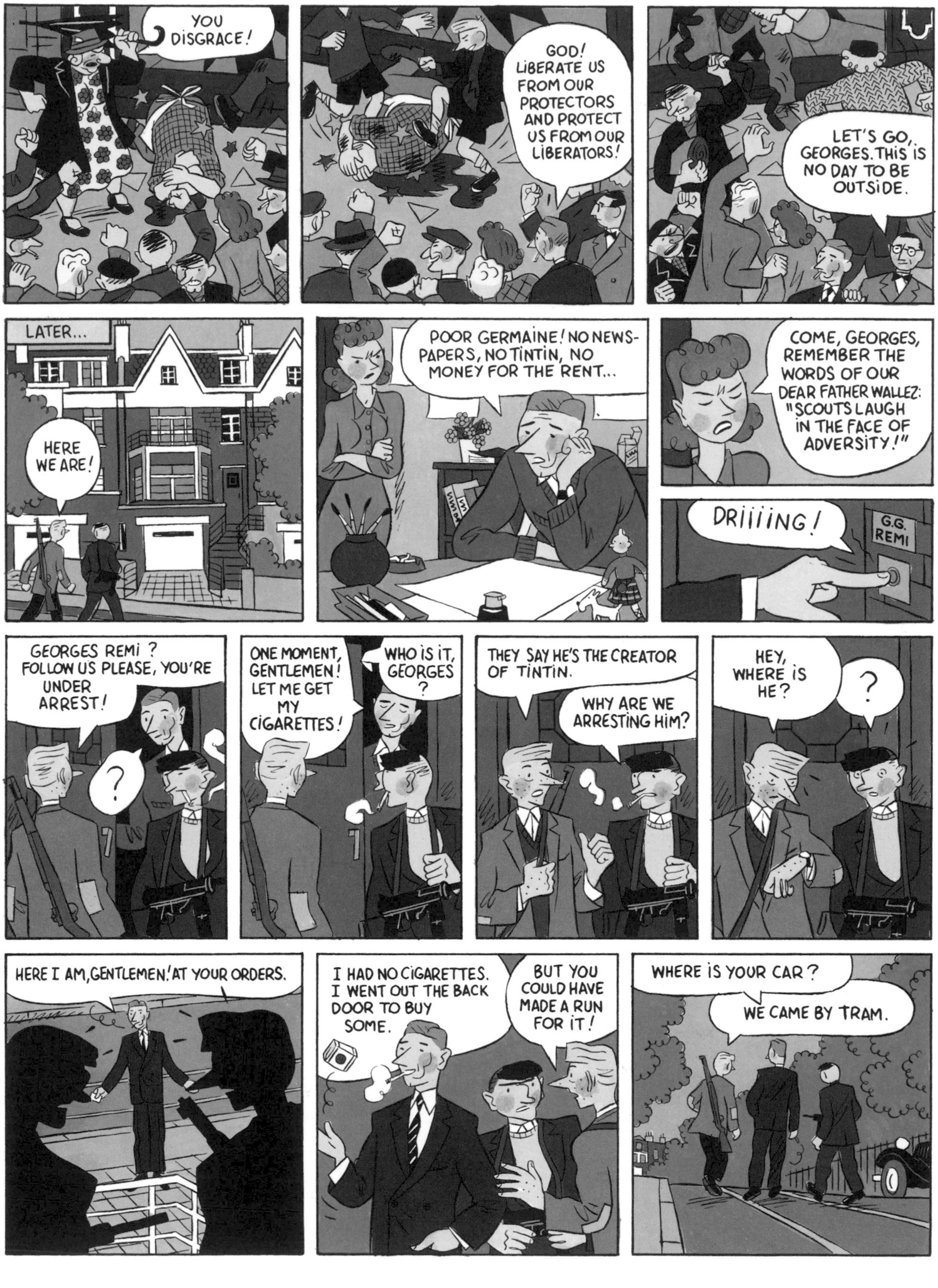
YOU DISGRACE!
GOD! LIBERATE US FROM OUR PROTECTORS AND PROTECT US FROM OUR LIBERATORS!
LET'S GO, GEORGES. THIS IS NO DAY TO BE OUTSIDE.
LATER...
HERE WE ARE!
POOR GERMAINE! NO NEWS-PAPERS, NO TINTIN, NO MONEY FOR THE RENT...
COME, GEORGES, REMEMBER THE WORDS OF OUR DEAR FATHER WALLEZ: "SCOUTS LAUGH IN THE FACE OF ADVERSITY!"
DRIIIING!
G.G. REMI
GEORGES REMI ? FOLLOW US PLEASE, YOU'RE UNDER ARREST!
?
ONE MOMENT, GENTLEMEN! LET ME GET MY CIGARETTES!
WHO IS IT, GEORGES ?
THEY SAY HE'S THE CREATOR OF TINTIN.
WHY ARE WE ARRESTING HIM?
HEY, WHERE IS HE?
?
HERE I AM, GENTLEMEN! AT YOUR ORDERS.
I HAD NO CIGARETTES. I WENT OUT THE BACK DOOR TO BUY SOME.
BUT YOU COULD HAVE MADE A RUN FOR IT!
WHERE IS YOUR CAR?
WE CAME BY TRAM.

DRIING !

EDGAR ! I'M TERRIBLY WORRIED! THEY'VE ARRESTED GEORGES AGAIN. THIS IS THE FOURTH TIME...

SAINT-GILLES PRISON? POOR FELLOW!

AIM... FIRE!

BANG BANG BANG !!!

DEATH TO COMMUNIST PIGS

LONG LIVE THE KING!

SENTENCING PEOPLE FOR WORDS! AND YOU? WHY ARE THEY AFTER YOU?

FOR HAVING CONTRIBUTED TO THE "STOLEN" SOIR. I'M HERGÉ, THE AUTHOR OF TINTIN.

DEATH TO COMMUNIST PIGS

VE THE KING!

TINTIN IN PRISON! THE IMBECILES! THEY'LL GIVE US TEN YEARS, YOU'LL SEE! THEY'RE CRAZY!

COUNCIL OF THE RESISTANCE.

GENTLEMEN, LET'S MOVE ON TO THE CASE OF REMI...

I INSIST ON A STRICT APPLICATION OF THE RULES."ALL WRITERS HAVING CONTRIBUTED TO A NEWSPAPER DURING THE OCCUPATION SHALL BE BARRED FROM EXCERCISING THEIR PROFESSION"...

IS JUSTICE SERVED BY AN ATTACK ON THE AUTHOR OF A BENIGN CHILDREN'S COMIC?

ABSOLUTELY! THIS TRAITOR'S COLLABORATIONIST VENOM POISONED OUR CHILDREN!

THAT'S RIDICULOUS! TINTIN IS A MODEL FOR BELGIAN YOUTH! WE HAVE NO RIGHT TO DESTROY HIM!

I EXPECTED NOTHING LESS FROM A LEOPOLDIST, LEBLANC!

DOGMATIC ASS! COMMUNIST!

GENTLEMEN, CALM DOWN!

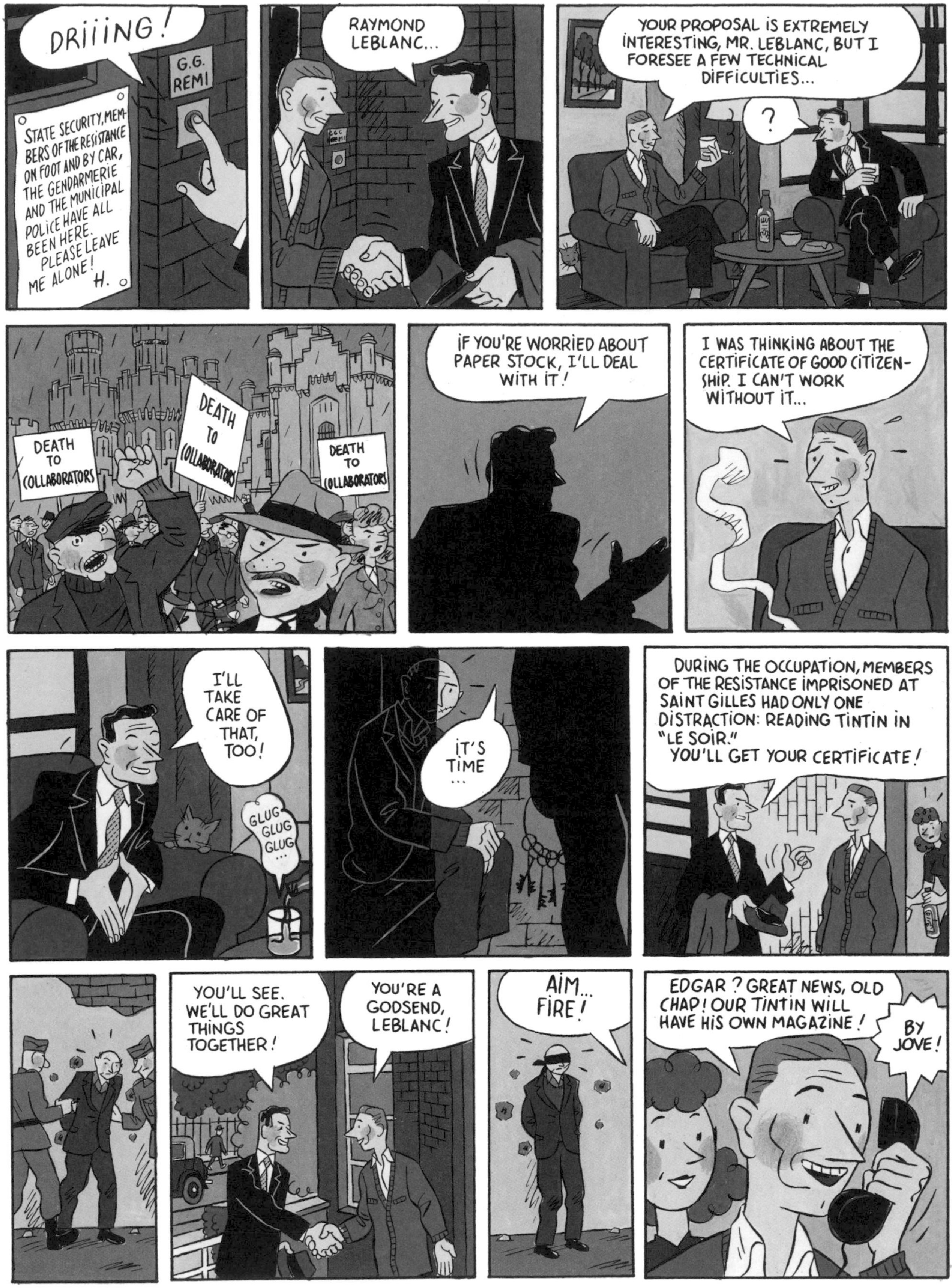
DRIiiNG!
G.G. REMI
STATE SECURITY, MEMBERS OF THE RESISTANCE ON FOOT AND BY CAR, THE GENDARMERIE AND THE MUNICIPAL POLICE HAVE ALL BEEN HERE. PLEASE LEAVE ME ALONE! H.
RAYMOND LEBLANC...
YOUR PROPOSAL IS EXTREMELY INTERESTING, MR. LEBLANC, BUT I FORESEE A FEW TECHNICAL DIFFICULTIES...
?
DEATH TO COLLABORATORS
DEATH TO COLLABORATORS
DEATH TO COLLABORATORS
IF YOU'RE WORRIED ABOUT PAPER STOCK, I'LL DEAL WITH IT!
I WAS THINKING ABOUT THE CERTIFICATE OF GOOD CITIZENSHIP. I CAN'T WORK WITHOUT IT...
I'LL TAKE CARE OF THAT, TOO!
GLUG GLUG GLUG...
IT'S TIME...
DURING THE OCCUPATION, MEMBERS OF THE RESISTANCE IMPRISONED AT SAINT GILLES HAD ONLY ONE DISTRACTION: READING TINTIN IN "LE SOIR." YOU'LL GET YOUR CERTIFICATE!
YOU'LL SEE. WE'LL DO GREAT THINGS TOGETHER!
YOU'RE A GODSEND, LEBLANC!
AIM... FIRE!
EDGAR? GREAT NEWS, OLD CHAP! OUR TINTIN WILL HAVE HIS OWN MAGAZINE!
BY JOVE!

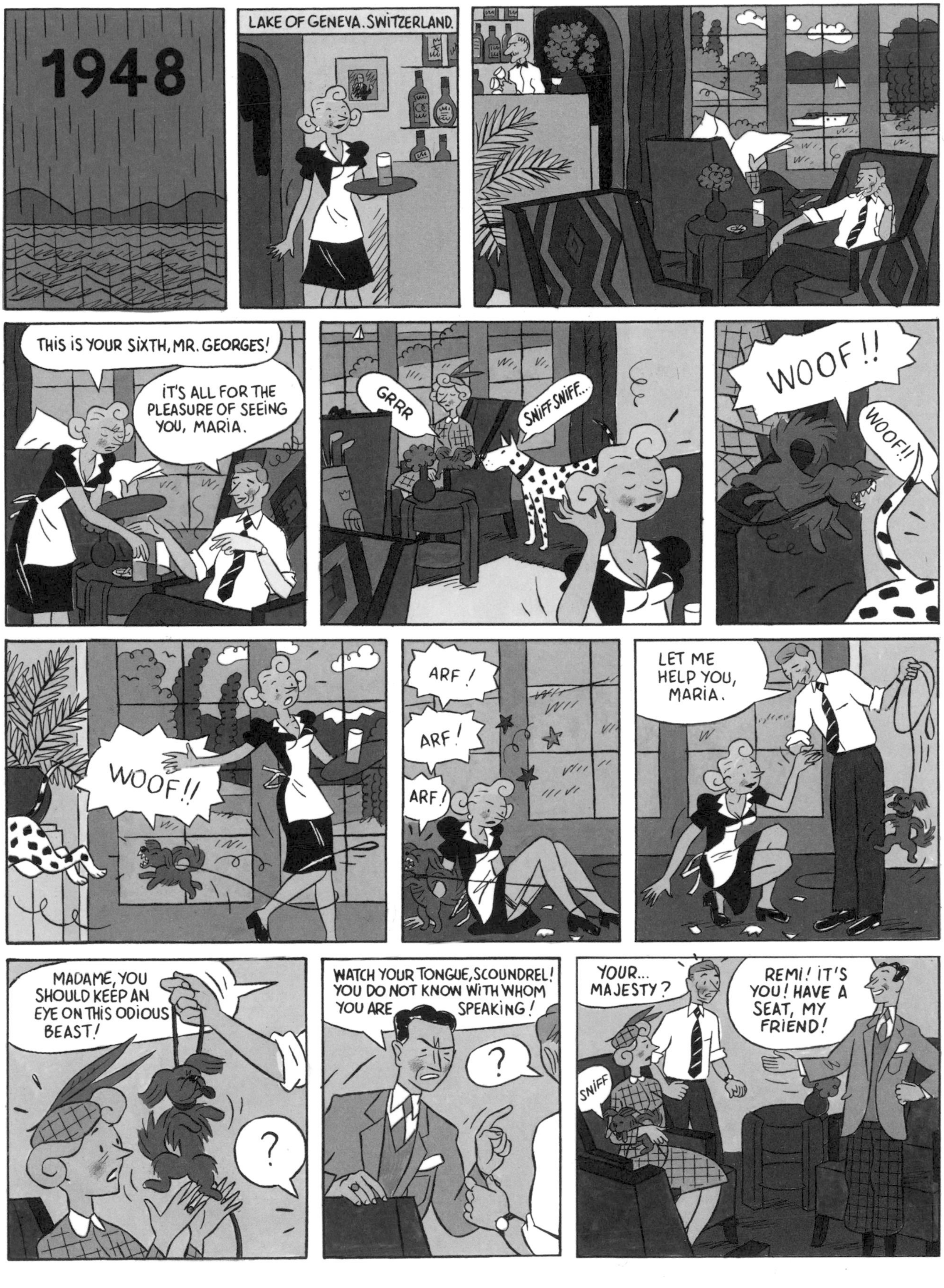
1948
LAKE OF GENEVA. SWITZERLAND.
THIS IS YOUR SIXTH, MR. GEORGES!
IT'S ALL FOR THE PLEASURE OF SEEING YOU, MARIA.
GRRR
SNIFF SNIFF...
WOOF!!
WOOF!!
WOOF!!
ARF!
ARF!
ARF!
LET ME HELP YOU, MARIA.
MADAME, YOU SHOULD KEEP AN EYE ON THIS ODIOUS BEAST!
?
WATCH YOUR TONGUE, SCOUNDREL! YOU DO NOT KNOW WITH WHOM YOU ARE SPEAKING!
?
YOUR... MAJESTY?
REMI! IT'S YOU! HAVE A SEAT, MY FRIEND!
SNIFF

SO, YOU'RE HERE, TOO, MENDING POSTWAR WOUNDS.

YES... IN A WAY, YOUR HIGHNESS.

GRRARR

BRUSSELS.

GOTFERDOUME!

"GOTFERDOUME"? YES, SIR, I'VE TAKEN NOTE.

DRING

DRING

TINTIN

BOOM BOOM BOOM

THAT WAS THE SIXTY-SEVENTH READER TO CALL TODAY. I DON'T KNOW WHAT TO TELL THEM, MR. LEBLANC!

?

REDAC... CHIEF

SHE'S RIGHT, RAYMOND. THIS CAN'T GO ON!

WE HAVE TO FIND GEORGES!

LE TEM... SOLEI...

IF HE DOESN'T DELIVER A SEQUEL TO THE TEMPLE, THE MAGAZINE IS DOOMED.

EMPI...

CALM DOWN, FRIENDS. AFTER ALL, I CAN'T PUT INTERPOL ON HIS HEELS.

WE'VE PREPARED THIS TO HELP OUR YOUNG READERS WAIT ...

Shocking news!
HERGÉ HAS DISAPPEARED

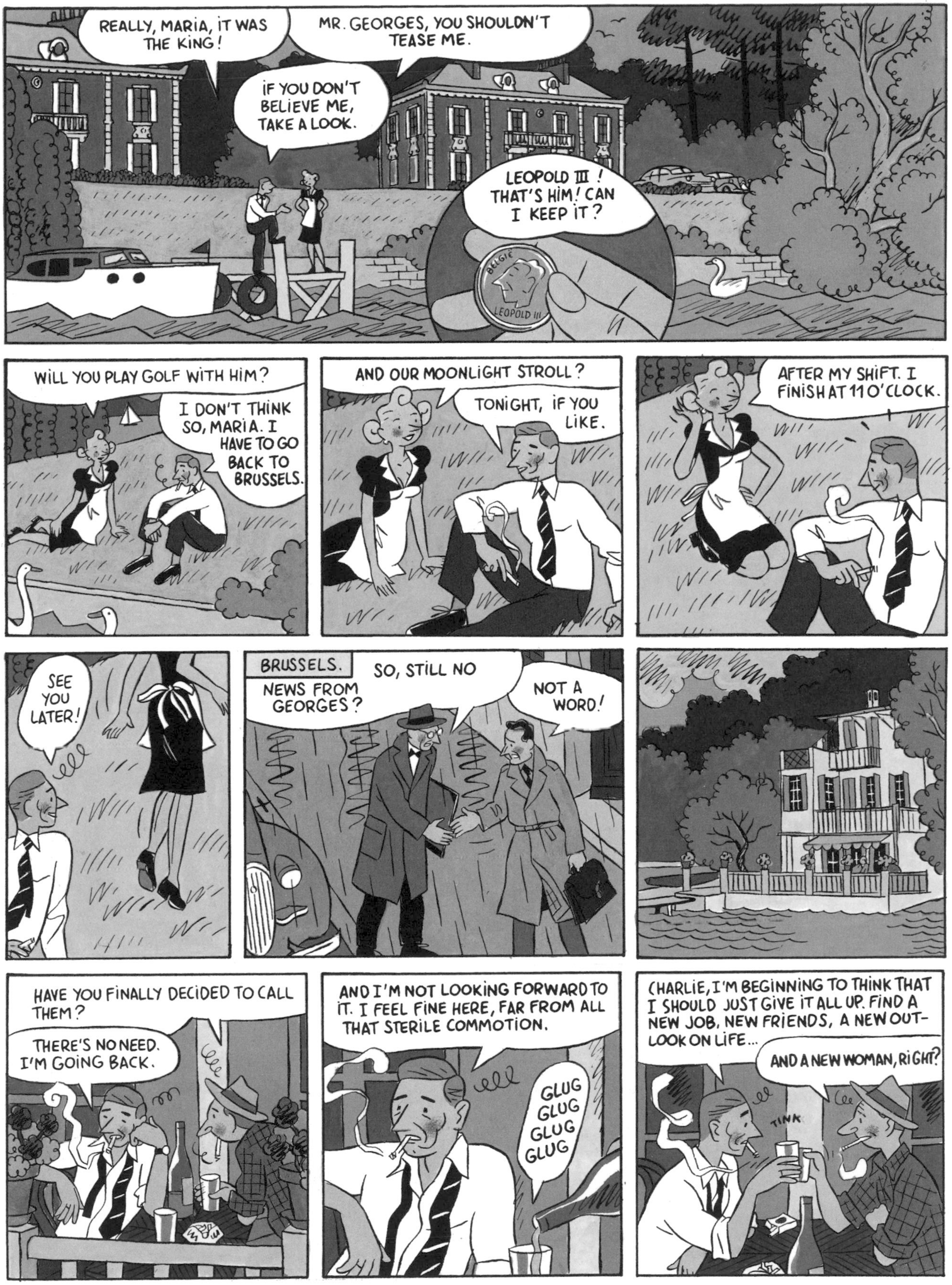
REALLY, MARIA, IT WAS THE KING!
MR. GEORGES, YOU SHOULDN'T TEASE ME.
IF YOU DON'T BELIEVE ME, TAKE A LOOK.
LEOPOLD III! THAT'S HIM! CAN I KEEP IT?
BELGIË
LEOPOLD III
WILL YOU PLAY GOLF WITH HIM?
I DON'T THINK SO, MARIA. I HAVE TO GO BACK TO BRUSSELS.
AND OUR MOONLIGHT STROLL?
TONIGHT, IF YOU LIKE.
AFTER MY SHIFT. I FINISH AT 11 O'CLOCK.
SEE YOU LATER!
BRUSSELS.
SO, STILL NO NEWS FROM GEORGES?
NOT A WORD!
HAVE YOU FINALLY DECIDED TO CALL THEM?
THERE'S NO NEED. I'M GOING BACK.
AND I'M NOT LOOKING FORWARD TO IT. I FEEL FINE HERE, FAR FROM ALL THAT STERILE COMMOTION.
GLUG GLUG GLUG GLUG
CHARLIE, I'M BEGINNING TO THINK THAT I SHOULD JUST GIVE IT ALL UP. FIND A NEW JOB, NEW FRIENDS, A NEW OUTLOOK ON LIFE...
AND A NEW WOMAN, RIGHT?
TINK

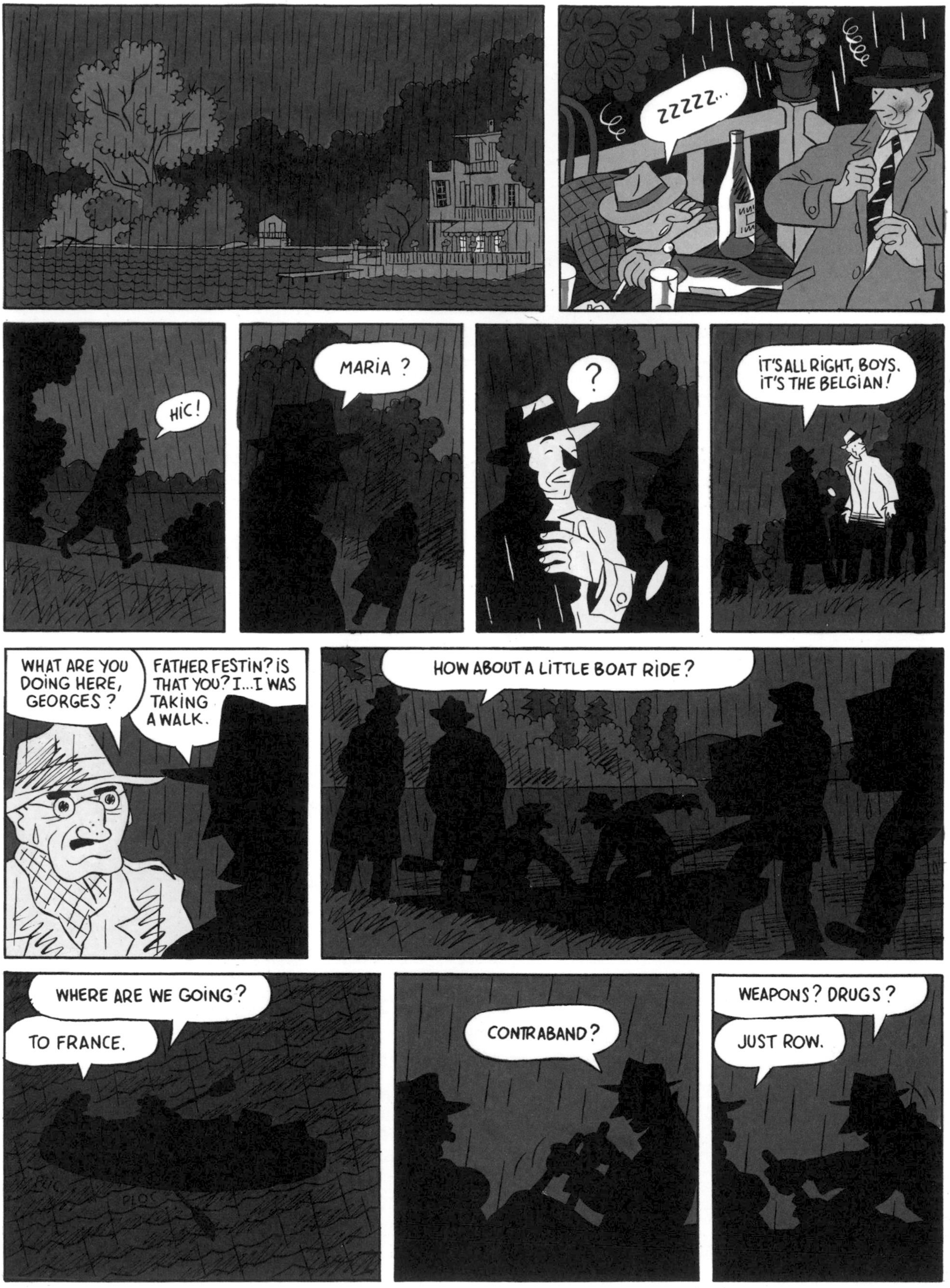
ZZZZZ...
HIC!
MARIA ?
?
IT'S ALL RIGHT, BOYS. IT'S THE BELGIAN!
WHAT ARE YOU DOING HERE, GEORGES ?
FATHER FESTIN? IS THAT YOU? I...I WAS TAKING A WALK.
HOW ABOUT A LITTLE BOAT RIDE?
WHERE ARE WE GOING?
TO FRANCE.
CONTRABAND?
WEAPONS? DRUGS?
JUST ROW.

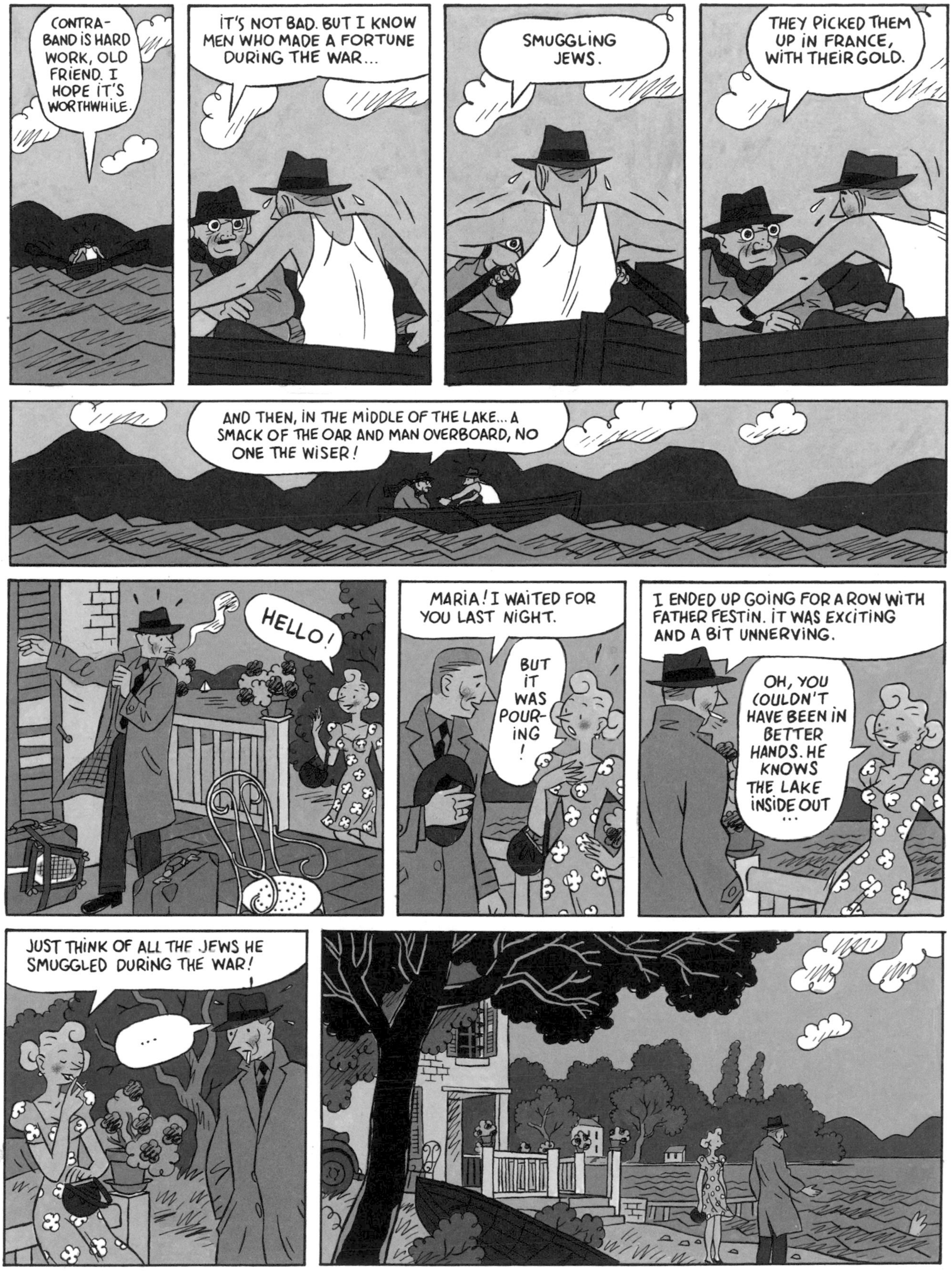
CONTRA-BAND IS HARD WORK, OLD FRIEND. I HOPE IT'S WORTHWHILE.
IT'S NOT BAD. BUT I KNOW MEN WHO MADE A FORTUNE DURING THE WAR...
SMUGGLING JEWS.
THEY PICKED THEM UP IN FRANCE, WITH THEIR GOLD.
AND THEN, IN THE MIDDLE OF THE LAKE... A SMACK OF THE OAR AND MAN OVERBOARD, NO ONE THE WISER!
HELLO!
MARIA! I WAITED FOR YOU LAST NIGHT.
BUT IT WAS POUR-ING!
I ENDED UP GOING FOR A ROW WITH FATHER FESTIN. IT WAS EXCITING AND A BIT UNNERVING.
OH, YOU COULDN'T HAVE BEEN IN BETTER HANDS. HE KNOWS THE LAKE INSIDE OUT...
JUST THINK OF ALL THE JEWS HE SMUGGLED DURING THE WAR!
...

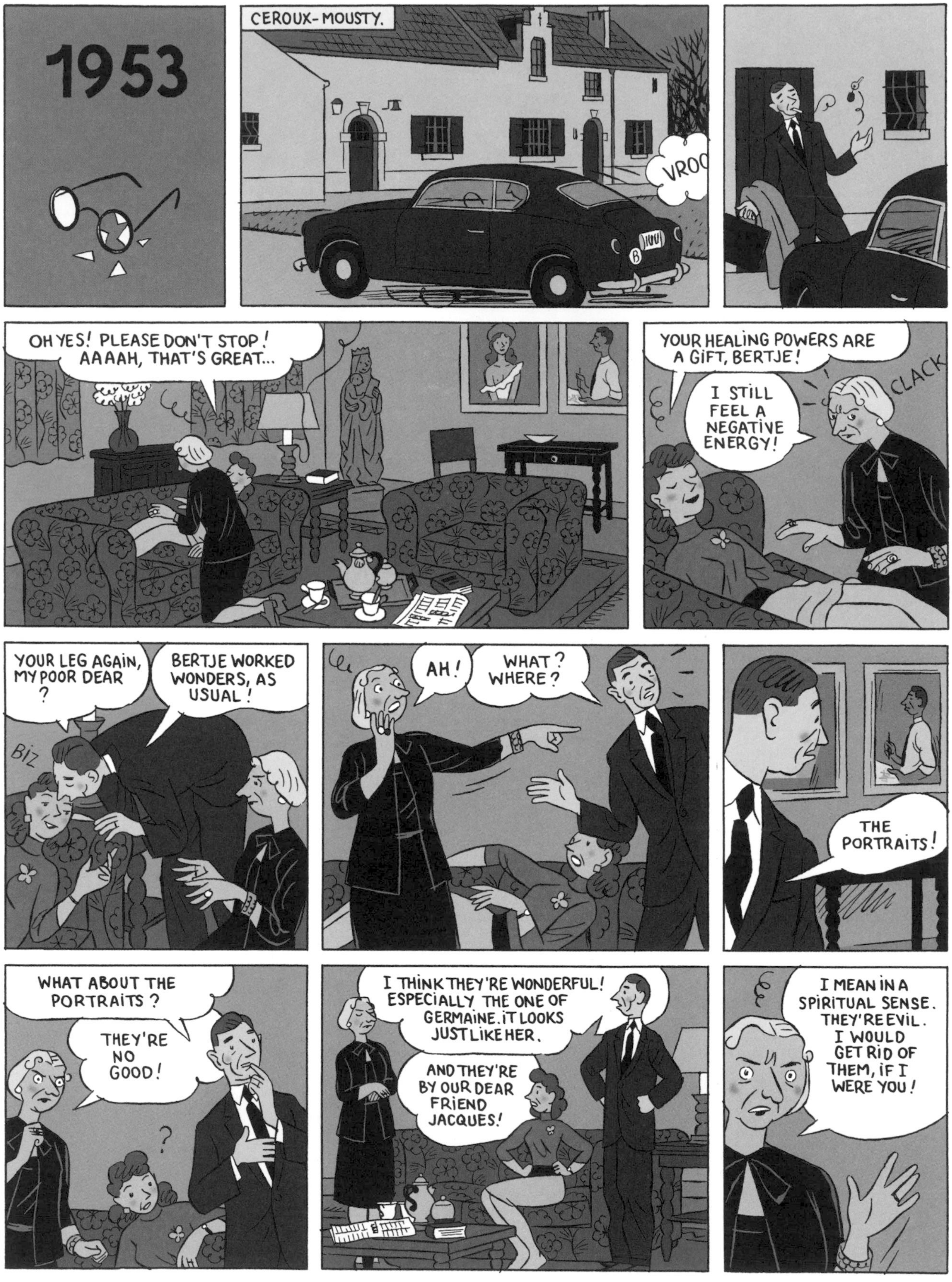
1953
CEROUX-MOUSTY.
VROO
OH YES! PLEASE DON'T STOP! AAAAH, THAT'S GREAT...
YOUR HEALING POWERS ARE A GIFT, BERTJE!
I STILL FEEL A NEGATIVE ENERGY!
CLACK
YOUR LEG AGAIN, MY POOR DEAR?
BERTJE WORKED WONDERS, AS USUAL!
BIZ
AH!
WHAT? WHERE?
THE PORTRAITS!
WHAT ABOUT THE PORTRAITS?
THEY'RE NO GOOD!
?
I THINK THEY'RE WONDERFUL! ESPECIALLY THE ONE OF GERMAINE. IT LOOKS JUST LIKE HER.
AND THEY'RE BY OUR DEAR FRIEND JACQUES!
I MEAN IN A SPIRITUAL SENSE. THEY'RE EVIL. I WOULD GET RID OF THEM, IF I WERE YOU!

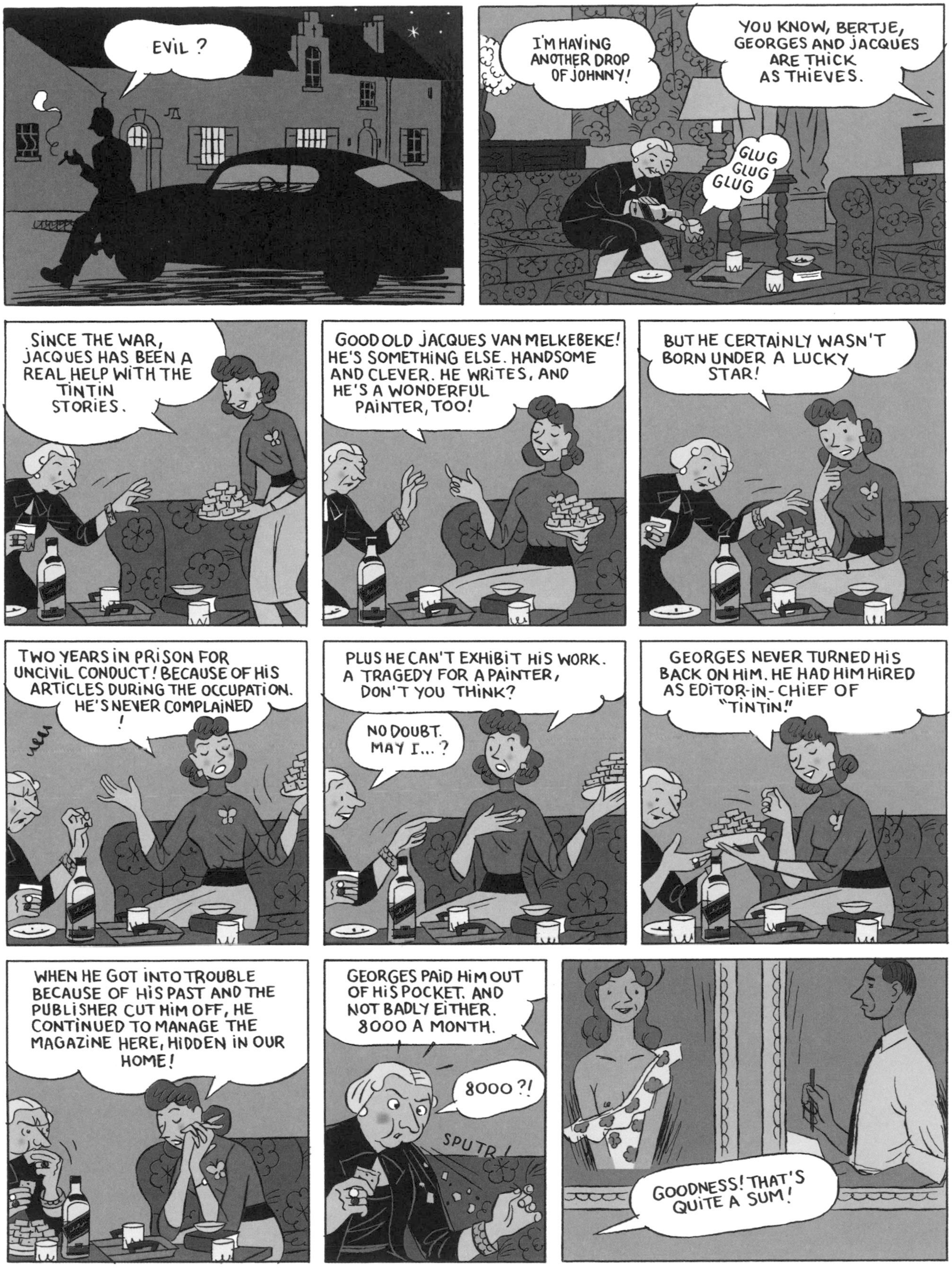
EVIL ?
I'M HAVING ANOTHER DROP OF JOHNNY!
YOU KNOW, BERTJE, GEORGES AND JACQUES ARE THICK AS THIEVES.
GLUG GLUG GLUG
SINCE THE WAR, JACQUES HAS BEEN A REAL HELP WITH THE TINTIN STORIES.
GOOD OLD JACQUES VAN MELKEBEKE! HE'S SOMETHING ELSE. HANDSOME AND CLEVER. HE WRITES, AND HE'S A WONDERFUL PAINTER, TOO!
BUT HE CERTAINLY WASN'T BORN UNDER A LUCKY STAR!
TWO YEARS IN PRISON FOR UNCIVIL CONDUCT! BECAUSE OF HIS ARTICLES DURING THE OCCUPATION. HE'S NEVER COMPLAINED!
PLUS HE CAN'T EXHIBIT HIS WORK. A TRAGEDY FOR A PAINTER, DON'T YOU THINK?
NO DOUBT. MAY I...?
GEORGES NEVER TURNED HIS BACK ON HIM. HE HAD HIM HIRED AS EDITOR-IN-CHIEF OF "TINTIN."
WHEN HE GOT INTO TROUBLE BECAUSE OF HIS PAST AND THE PUBLISHER CUT HIM OFF, HE CONTINUED TO MANAGE THE MAGAZINE HERE, HIDDEN IN OUR HOME!
GEORGES PAID HIM OUT OF HIS POCKET. AND NOT BADLY EITHER. 8000 A MONTH.
8000 ?!
SPUTR!
GOODNESS! THAT'S QUITE A SUM!

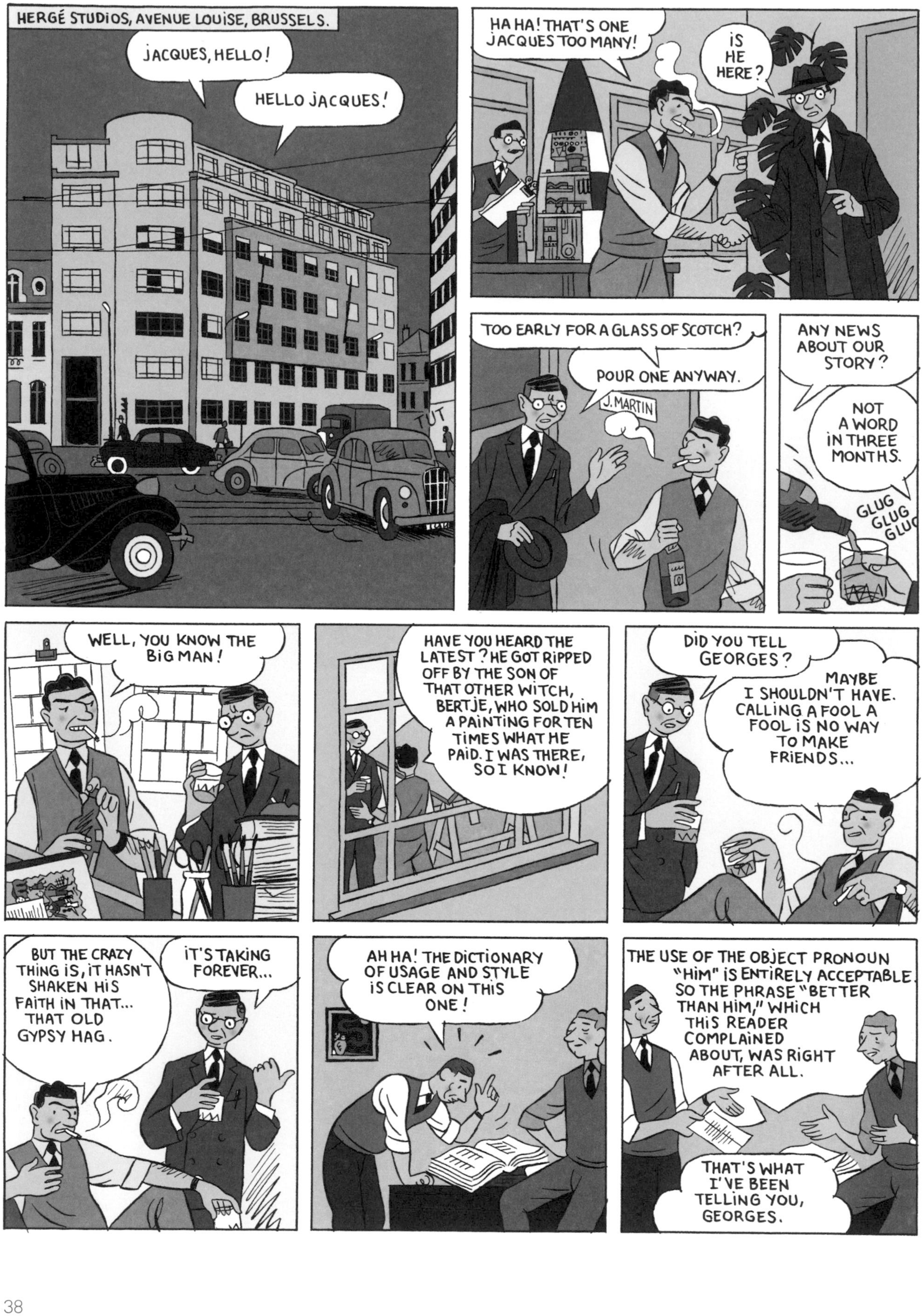

HERGÉ STUDIOS, AVENUE LOUISE, BRUSSELS.
JACQUES, HELLO!
HELLO JACQUES!
TUT
HA HA! THAT'S ONE JACQUES TOO MANY!
IS HE HERE?
TOO EARLY FOR A GLASS OF SCOTCH?
POUR ONE ANYWAY.
J. MARTIN
ANY NEWS ABOUT OUR STORY?
NOT A WORD IN THREE MONTHS.
GLUG GLUG GLUG
WELL, YOU KNOW THE BIG MAN!
HAVE YOU HEARD THE LATEST? HE GOT RIPPED OFF BY THE SON OF THAT OTHER WITCH, BERTJE, WHO SOLD HIM A PAINTING FOR TEN TIMES WHAT HE PAID. I WAS THERE, SO I KNOW!
DID YOU TELL GEORGES?
MAYBE I SHOULDN'T HAVE. CALLING A FOOL A FOOL IS NO WAY TO MAKE FRIENDS...
BUT THE CRAZY THING IS, IT HASN'T SHAKEN HIS FAITH IN THAT... THAT OLD GYPSY HAG.
IT'S TAKING FOREVER...
AH HA! THE DICTIONARY OF USAGE AND STYLE IS CLEAR ON THIS ONE!
THE USE OF THE OBJECT PRONOUN "HIM" IS ENTIRELY ACCEPTABLE. SO THE PHRASE "BETTER THAN HIM," WHICH THIS READER COMPLAINED ABOUT, WAS RIGHT AFTER ALL.
THAT'S WHAT I'VE BEEN TELLING YOU, GEORGES.

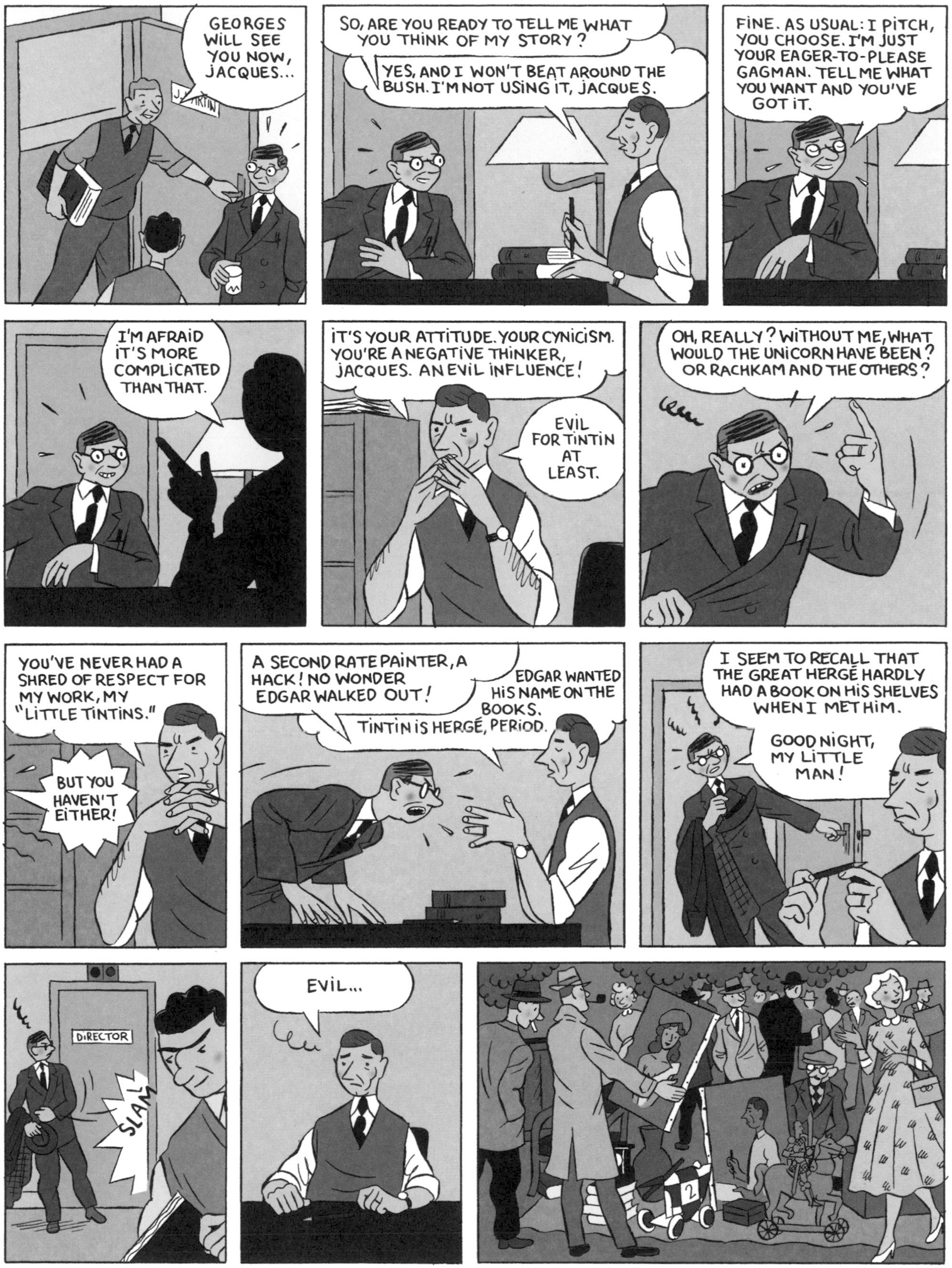
GEORGES WILL SEE YOU NOW, JACQUES...
SO, ARE YOU READY TO TELL ME WHAT YOU THINK OF MY STORY?
YES, AND I WON'T BEAT AROUND THE BUSH. I'M NOT USING IT, JACQUES.
FINE. AS USUAL: I PITCH, YOU CHOOSE. I'M JUST YOUR EAGER-TO-PLEASE GAGMAN. TELL ME WHAT YOU WANT AND YOU'VE GOT IT.
I'M AFRAID IT'S MORE COMPLICATED THAN THAT.
IT'S YOUR ATTITUDE. YOUR CYNICISM. YOU'RE A NEGATIVE THINKER, JACQUES. AN EVIL INFLUENCE!
EVIL FOR TINTIN AT LEAST.
OH, REALLY? WITHOUT ME, WHAT WOULD THE UNICORN HAVE BEEN? OR RACHKAM AND THE OTHERS?
YOU'VE NEVER HAD A SHRED OF RESPECT FOR MY WORK, MY "LITTLE TINTINS."
BUT YOU HAVEN'T EITHER!
A SECOND RATE PAINTER, A HACK! NO WONDER EDGAR WALKED OUT!
EDGAR WANTED HIS NAME ON THE BOOKS.
TINTIN IS HERGÉ, PERIOD.
I SEEM TO RECALL THAT THE GREAT HERGÉ HARDLY HAD A BOOK ON HIS SHELVES WHEN I MET HIM.
GOOD NIGHT, MY LITTLE MAN!
DIRECTOR
SLAM
EVIL...

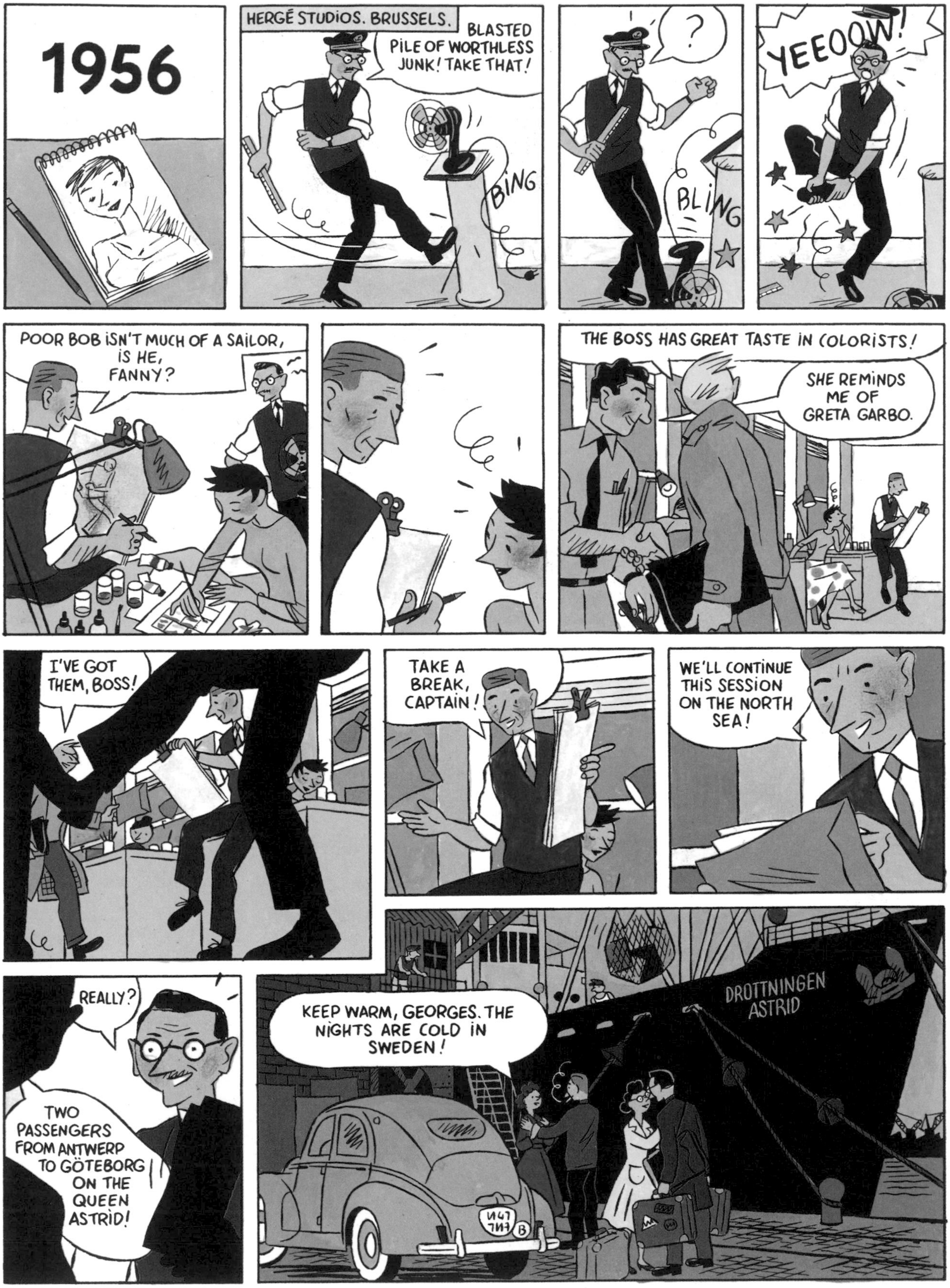
1956
HERGÉ STUDIOS. BRUSSELS.
BLASTED PILE OF WORTHLESS JUNK! TAKE THAT!
BING
?
BLING
YEEOOW!
POOR BOB ISN'T MUCH OF A SAILOR, IS HE, FANNY?
THE BOSS HAS GREAT TASTE IN COLORISTS!
SHE REMINDS ME OF GRETA GARBO.
I'VE GOT THEM, BOSS!
TAKE A BREAK, CAPTAIN!
WE'LL CONTINUE THIS SESSION ON THE NORTH SEA!
REALLY?
TWO PASSENGERS FROM ANTWERP TO GÖTEBORG ON THE QUEEN ASTRID!
KEEP WARM, GEORGES. THE NIGHTS ARE COLD IN SWEDEN!
DROTTNINGEN ASTRID

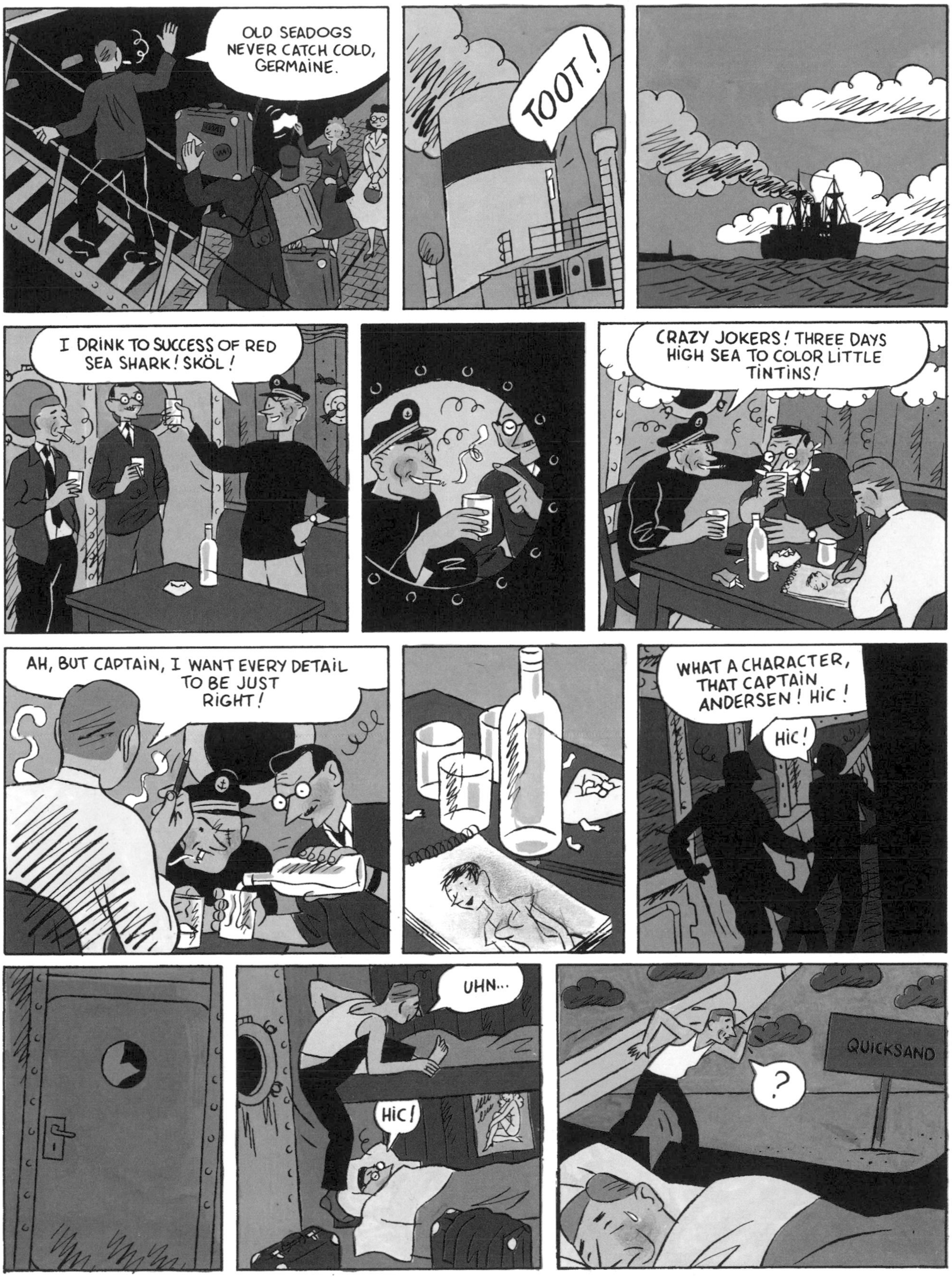

OLD SEADOGS NEVER CATCH COLD, GERMAINE.
TOOT!
I DRINK TO SUCCESS OF RED SEA SHARK! SKÖL!
CRAZY JOKERS! THREE DAYS HIGH SEA TO COLOR LITTLE TINTINS!
AH, BUT CAPTAIN, I WANT EVERY DETAIL TO BE JUST RIGHT!
WHAT A CHARACTER, THAT CAPTAIN ANDERSEN! HIC!
HIC!
UHN...
HIC!
QUICKSAND
?

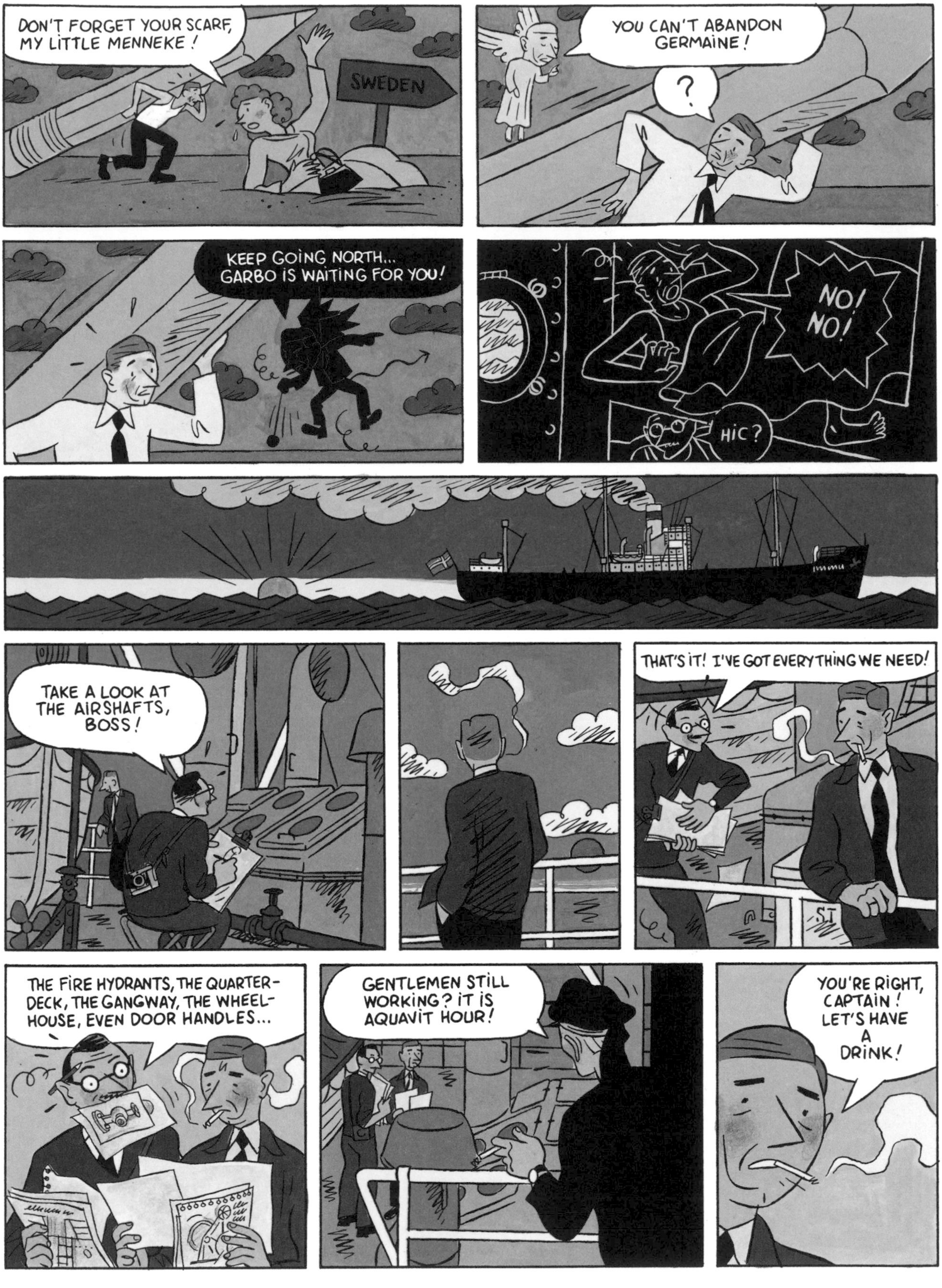
DON'T FORGET YOUR SCARF, MY LITTLE MENNEKE!
SWEDEN
YOU CAN'T ABANDON GERMAINE!
?
KEEP GOING NORTH... GARBO IS WAITING FOR YOU!
NO! NO!
HIC?
TAKE A LOOK AT THE AIRSHAFTS, BOSS!
THAT'S IT! I'VE GOT EVERYTHING WE NEED!
THE FIRE HYDRANTS, THE QUARTER-DECK, THE GANGWAY, THE WHEEL-HOUSE, EVEN DOOR HANDLES...
GENTLEMEN STILL WORKING? IT IS AQUAVIT HOUR!
YOU'RE RIGHT, CAPTAIN! LET'S HAVE A DRINK!

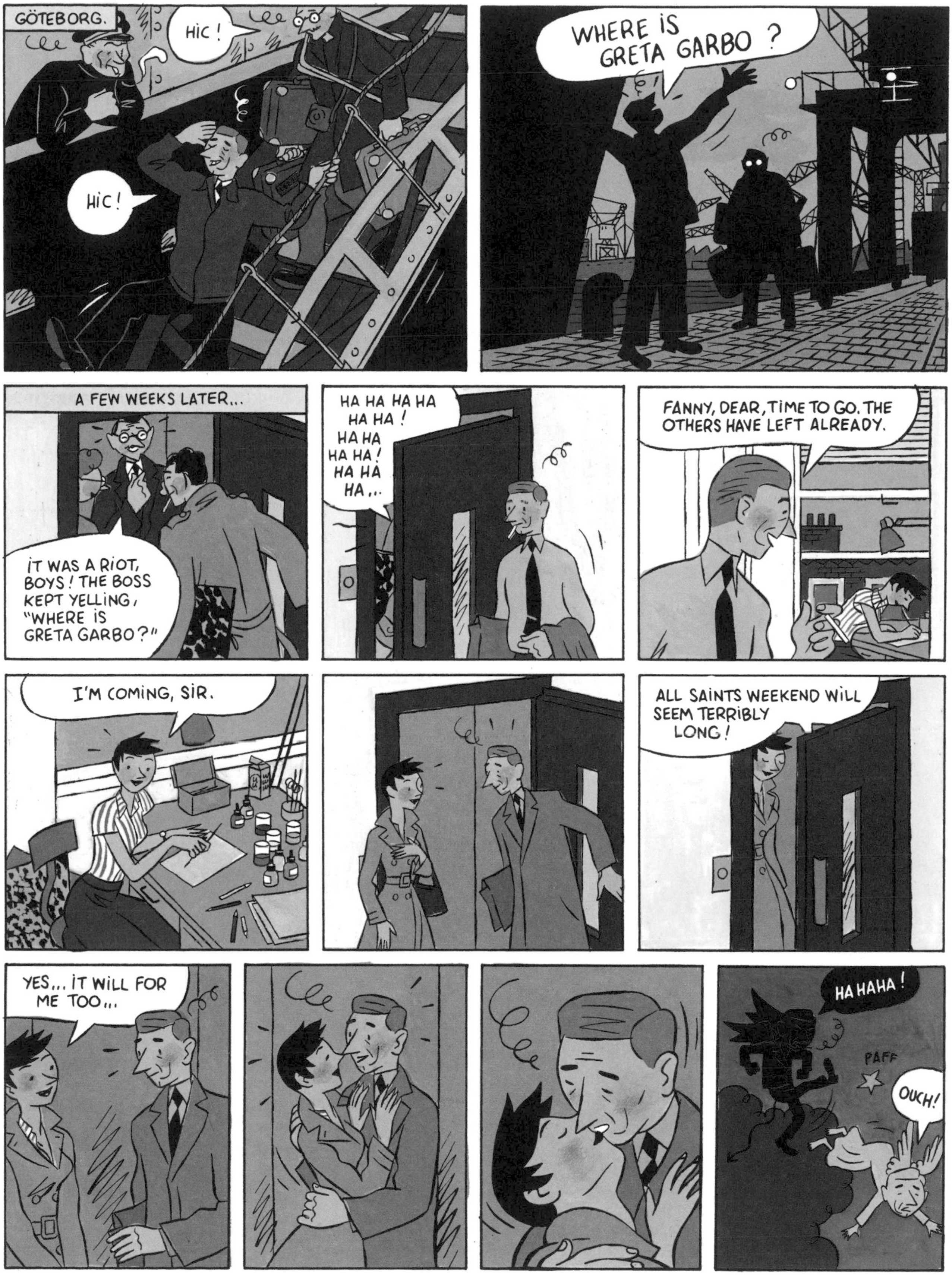
GÖTEBORG.
HIC !
HIC !
WHERE IS GRETA GARBO ?
A FEW WEEKS LATER...
IT WAS A RIOT, BOYS ! THE BOSS KEPT YELLING, "WHERE IS GRETA GARBO ?"
HA HA HA HA HA HA ! HA HA HA HA ! HA HA HA...
FANNY, DEAR, TIME TO GO. THE OTHERS HAVE LEFT ALREADY.
I'M COMING, SIR.
ALL SAINTS WEEKEND WILL SEEM TERRIBLY LONG !
YES... IT WILL FOR ME TOO...
HA HAHA !
PAFF
OUCH!

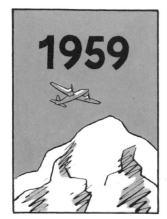

1959

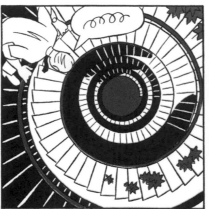

ZURICH.

I WAS TERRIFIED. I KNEW HE WANTED TO THROW ME INTO THE VOID. I HAD TO GO BACK UP, BUT HE WAS IN MY WAY. I COULDN'T GET BY!

THE NIGHTMARE ABOUT THE WHITE DEMON IS OBVIOUSLY RELATED TO YOUR CURRENT PROJECT.

WELL, MOST OF "TINTIN IN TIBET" DOES TAKE PLACE IN THE SNOW. THE CHARACTERS ARE TRACKING A YETI.

THE ABOMINABLE SNOWMAN... ANOTHER WHITE DEMON!

I DON'T WANT TO DISCOURAGE YOU, BUT YOU'LL NEVER FINISH THIS PROJECT. YOU HAVE TO FACE YOUR MARITAL CRISIS AS AN ADULT...

AND KILL THE DEMON OF PURITY WITHIN YOU!

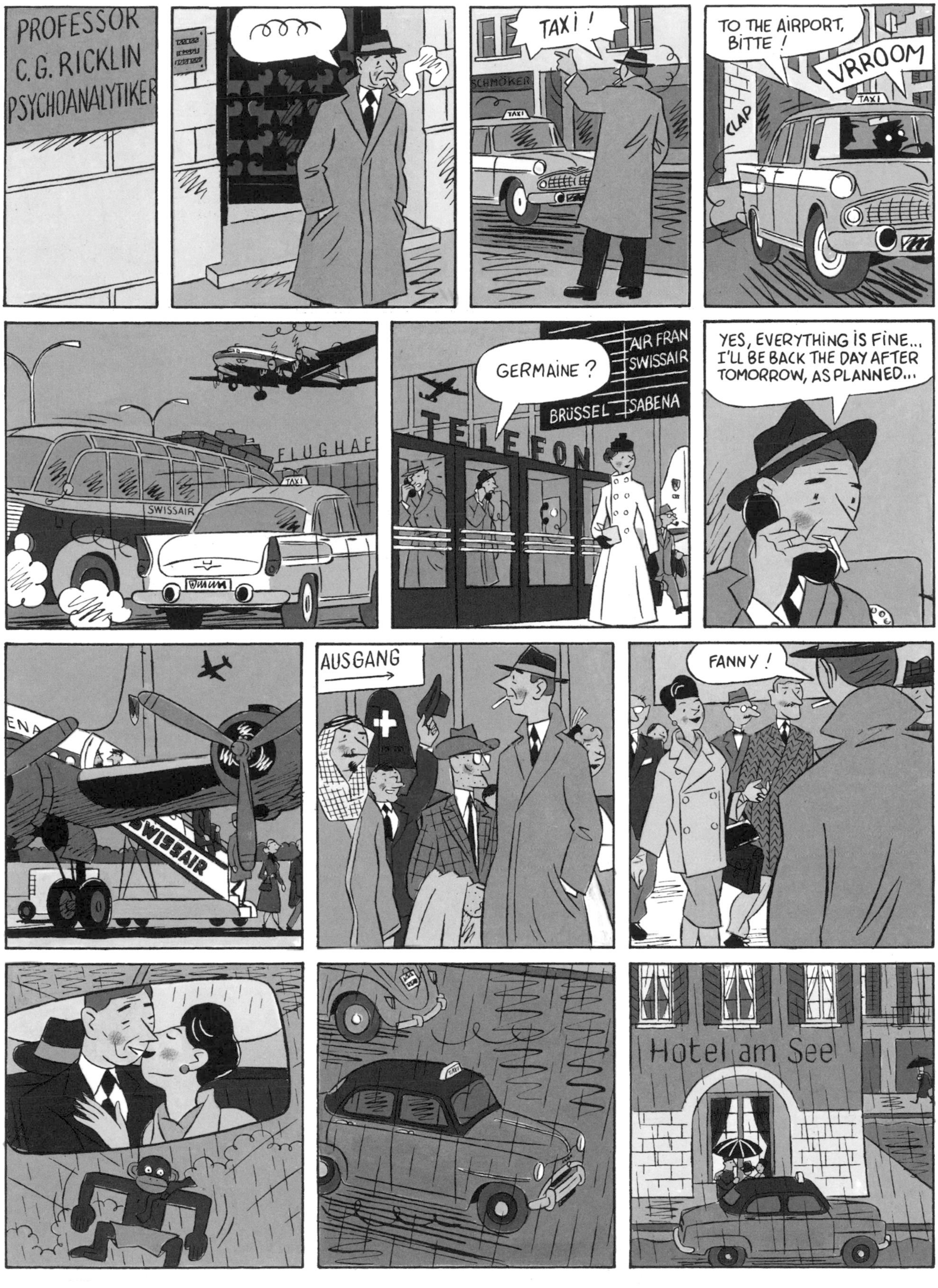
PROFESSOR
C. G. RICKLIN
PSYCHOANALYTIKER
TAXi !
SCHMÖKER
TAXI
TO THE AIRPORT, BITTE !
VRROOM
CLAP
TAXI
FLUGHAF
TAXI
SWISSAIR
AIR FRAN
SWISSAIR
BRÜSSEL
SABENA
GERMAINE ?
TELEFON
YES, EVERYTHING IS FINE... I'LL BE BACK THE DAY AFTER TOMORROW, AS PLANNED...
ENA
SWISSAIR
AUSGANG
FANNY !
Hotel am See

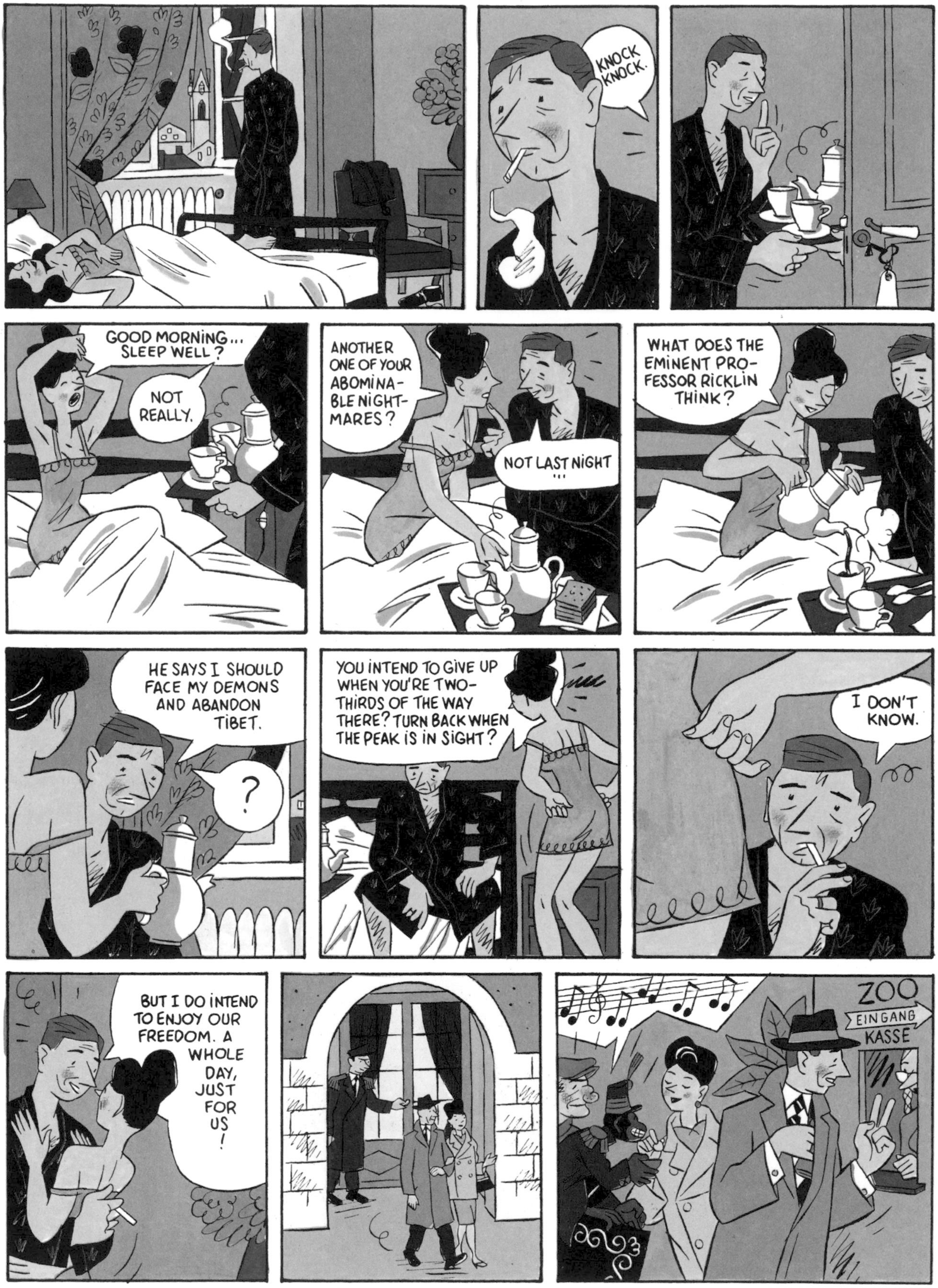
KNOCK KNOCK.
GOOD MORNING... SLEEP WELL?
NOT REALLY.
ANOTHER ONE OF YOUR ABOMINABLE NIGHTMARES?
NOT LAST NIGHT ...
WHAT DOES THE EMINENT PROFESSOR RICKLIN THINK?
HE SAYS I SHOULD FACE MY DEMONS AND ABANDON TIBET.
?
YOU INTEND TO GIVE UP WHEN YOU'RE TWO-THIRDS OF THE WAY THERE? TURN BACK WHEN THE PEAK IS IN SIGHT?
I DON'T KNOW.
BUT I DO INTEND TO ENJOY OUR FREEDOM. A WHOLE DAY, JUST FOR US!
ZOO
EINGANG
KASSE

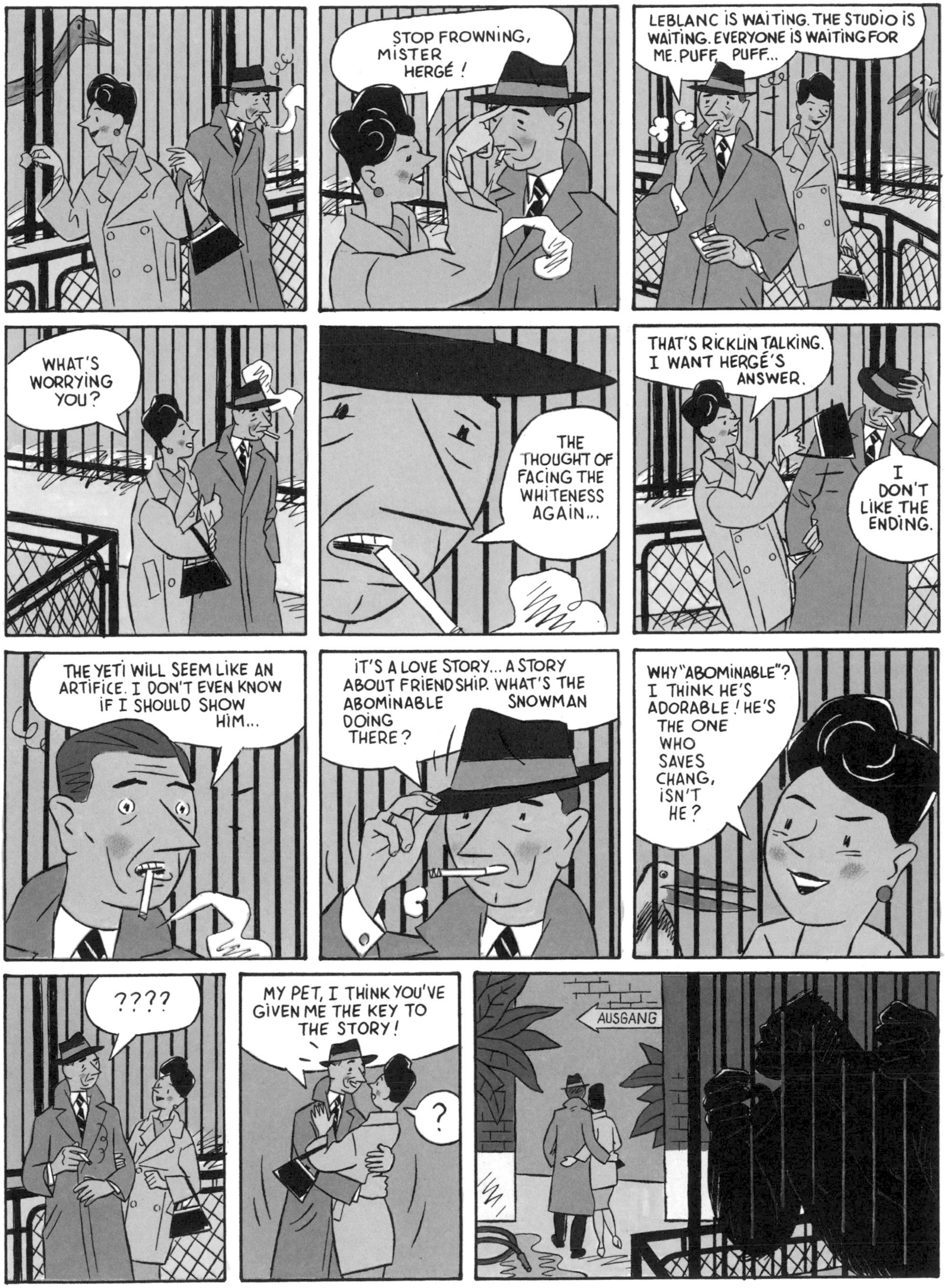
STOP FROWNING, MISTER HERGÉ !
LEBLANC IS WAITING. THE STUDIO IS WAITING. EVERYONE IS WAITING FOR ME. PUFF PUFF...
WHAT'S WORRYING YOU?
THE THOUGHT OF FACING THE WHITENESS AGAIN...
THAT'S RICKLIN TALKING. I WANT HERGÉ'S ANSWER.
I DON'T LIKE THE ENDING.
THE YETI WILL SEEM LIKE AN ARTIFICE. I DON'T EVEN KNOW IF I SHOULD SHOW HIM...
IT'S A LOVE STORY... A STORY ABOUT FRIENDSHIP. WHAT'S THE ABOMINABLE SNOWMAN DOING THERE?
WHY "ABOMINABLE"? I THINK HE'S ADORABLE! HE'S THE ONE WHO SAVES CHANG, ISN'T HE?
????
MY PET, I THINK YOU'VE GIVEN ME THE KEY TO THE STORY!
?
AUSGANG

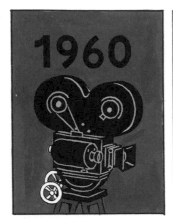

1960

BOULOGNE-BILLANCOURT.

STUDIO. CINÉMA.SA

LET'S STAND TALL, JEAN-PIERRE. STRAIGHT AS PINS!

LIKE TINTIN!

A HISTORIC MOMENT!

FLASH

ANOTHER ONE, MR. HERGÉ!

WOOF!

THANK YOU, GENTLEMEN! WE HAVE WORK TO DO NOW!

MR. HERGÉ, A FEW WORDS FOR RADIO LUXEMBOURG.

TINTIN ON THE BIG SCREEN: IT'S FINALLY HAPPENING?

HAVE A LOOK! WE'RE ABOUT TO SHOOT THE FIRST TAKES OF "TINTIN AND THE GOLDEN FLEECE."

WHEN DID YOU FIRST THINK OF MAKING A MOVIE?

IT'S BEEN IN THE BACK OF MY MIND FOR A LONG TIME. THERE WAS EVEN TALK OF CAPTAIN COUSTEAU FILMING RED RACKHAM.

"THE GOLDEN FLEECE" IS A NEW ADVENTURE?

YES. ANDRÉ BARRET, OUR PRODUCER, TALKED ME INTO CREATING AN ORIGINAL SCREENPLAY FOR THE FILM...

SIGNED HERGÉ?

NO, BUT I WAS HEAVILY INVOLVED IN REVISING THE FINAL SCRIPT.

JEAN-HENRI, STOP TOUCHING THE DOG!

I WANTED TINTIN TO BE TRUE TO CHARACTER, YOU SEE...

GRRR...

AND AS FOR YOU, ASIDE. I'VE TOLD IN THE MOVIE!

BUDDY, STEP YOU: I AM

THIS WAY, SIR.

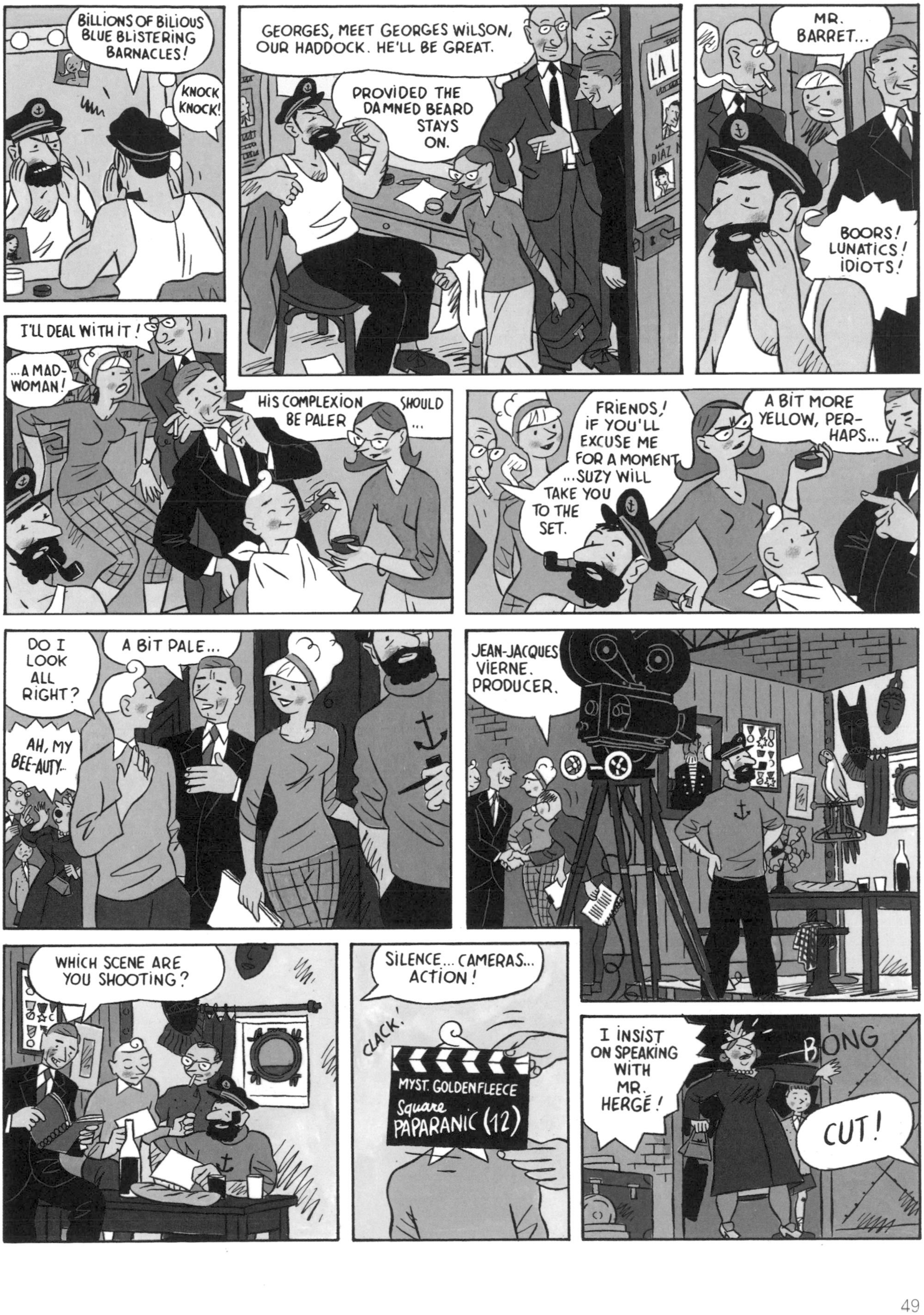

BILLIONS OF BILIOUS BLUE BLISTERING BARNACLES!
KNOCK KNOCK!
GEORGES, MEET GEORGES WILSON, OUR HADDOCK. HE'LL BE GREAT.
PROVIDED THE DAMNED BEARD STAYS ON.
MR. BARRET...
BOORS! LUNATICS! IDIOTS!
I'LL DEAL WITH IT!
...A MAD-WOMAN!
HIS COMPLEXION SHOULD BE PALER ...
FRIENDS! IF YOU'LL EXCUSE ME FOR A MOMENT ...SUZY WILL TAKE YOU TO THE SET.
A BIT MORE YELLOW, PER-HAPS...
DO I LOOK ALL RIGHT?
A BIT PALE...
AH, MY BEE-AUTY...
JEAN-JACQUES VIERNE. PRODUCER.
WHICH SCENE ARE YOU SHOOTING?
SILENCE... CAMERAS... ACTION!
CLACK!
MYST. GOLDENFLEECE
Square PAPARANIC (12)
I INSIST ON SPEAKING WITH MR. HERGÉ!
BONG
CUT!

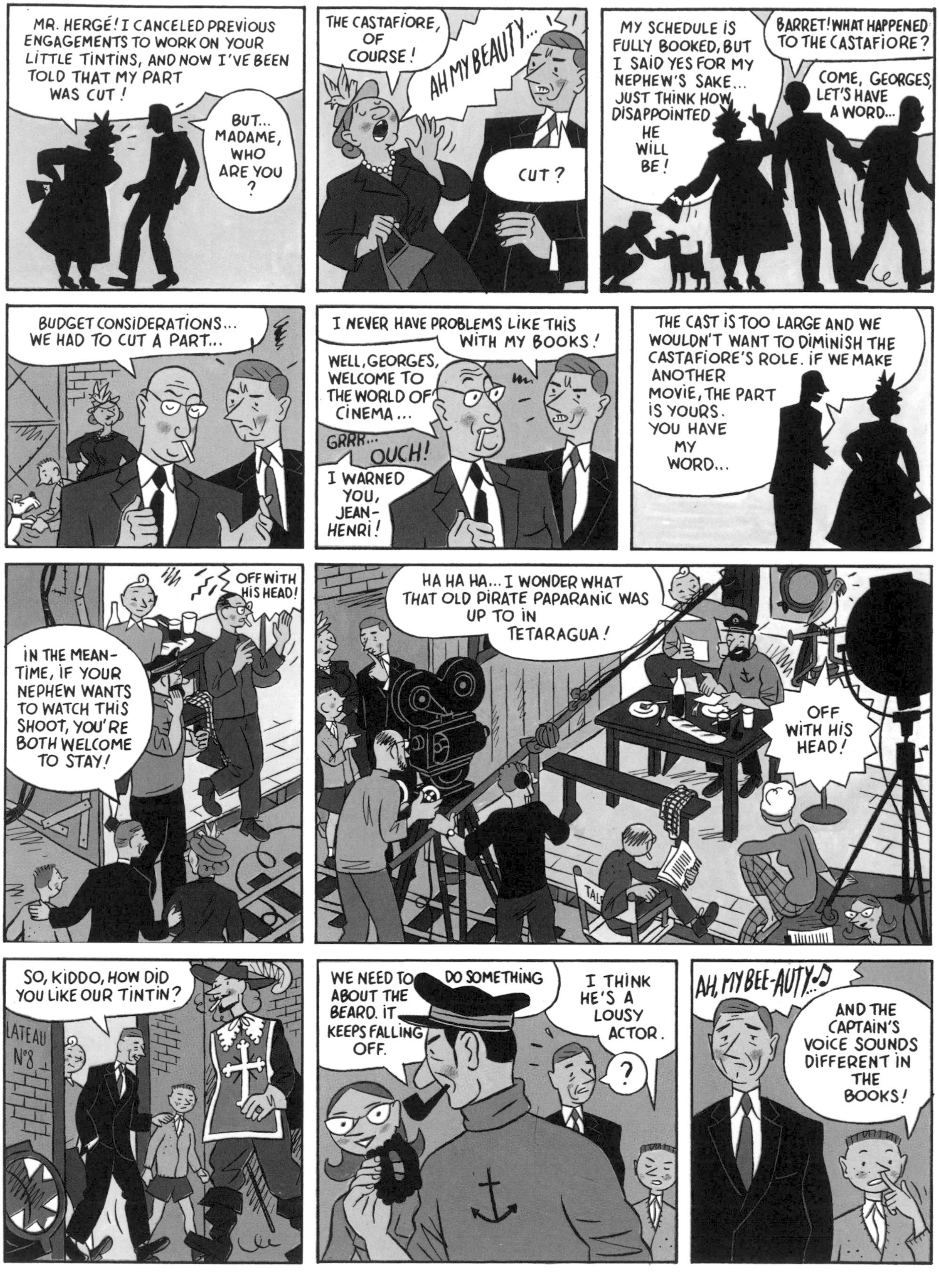
MR. HERGÉ! I CANCELED PREVIOUS ENGAGEMENTS TO WORK ON YOUR LITTLE TINTINS, AND NOW I'VE BEEN TOLD THAT MY PART WAS CUT!
BUT... MADAME, WHO ARE YOU?
THE CASTAFIORE, OF COURSE!
AH MY BEAUTY...
CUT?
MY SCHEDULE IS FULLY BOOKED, BUT I SAID YES FOR MY NEPHEW'S SAKE... JUST THINK HOW DISAPPOINTED HE WILL BE!
BARRET! WHAT HAPPENED TO THE CASTAFIORE?
COME, GEORGES, LET'S HAVE A WORD...
BUDGET CONSIDERATIONS... WE HAD TO CUT A PART...
I NEVER HAVE PROBLEMS LIKE THIS WITH MY BOOKS!
WELL, GEORGES, WELCOME TO THE WORLD OF CINEMA...
GRRR...
OUCH!
I WARNED YOU, JEAN-HENRI!
THE CAST IS TOO LARGE AND WE WOULDN'T WANT TO DIMINISH THE CASTAFIORE'S ROLE. IF WE MAKE ANOTHER MOVIE, THE PART IS YOURS. YOU HAVE MY WORD...
OFF WITH HIS HEAD!
IN THE MEANTIME, IF YOUR NEPHEW WANTS TO WATCH THIS SHOOT, YOU'RE BOTH WELCOME TO STAY!
HA HA HA... I WONDER WHAT THAT OLD PIRATE PAPARANIC WAS UP TO IN TETARAGUA!
OFF WITH HIS HEAD!
SO, KIDDO, HOW DID YOU LIKE OUR TINTIN?
LATEAU N°8
WE NEED TO DO SOMETHING ABOUT THE BEARD. IT KEEPS FALLING OFF.
I THINK HE'S A LOUSY ACTOR.
?
AH, MY BEE-AUTY!...
AND THE CAPTAIN'S VOICE SOUNDS DIFFERENT IN THE BOOKS!

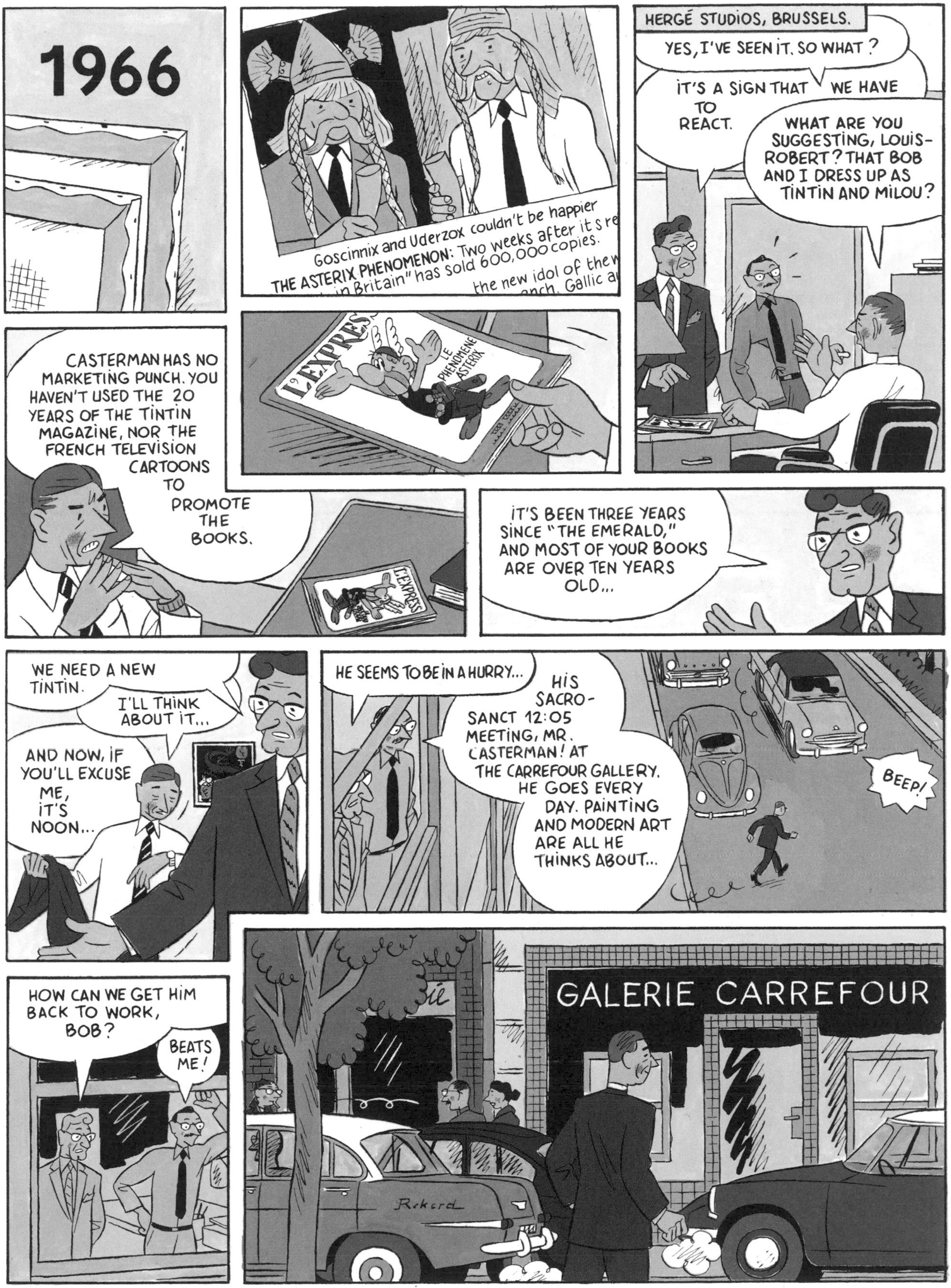
1966
Goscinnix and Uderzox couldn't be happier
THE ASTERIX PHENOMENON: Two weeks after it's re
"in Britain" has sold 600,000 copies.
the new idol of the w
HERGÉ STUDIOS, BRUSSELS.
YES, I'VE SEEN IT. SO WHAT?
IT'S A SIGN THAT WE HAVE TO REACT.
WHAT ARE YOU SUGGESTING, LOUIS-ROBERT? THAT BOB AND I DRESS UP AS TINTIN AND MILOU?
L'EXPRESS
LE PHÉNOMÈNE ASTÉRIX
CASTERMAN HAS NO MARKETING PUNCH. YOU HAVEN'T USED THE 20 YEARS OF THE TINTIN MAGAZINE, NOR THE FRENCH TELEVISION CARTOONS TO PROMOTE THE BOOKS.
L'EXPRESS
IT'S BEEN THREE YEARS SINCE "THE EMERALD," AND MOST OF YOUR BOOKS ARE OVER TEN YEARS OLD...
WE NEED A NEW TINTIN.
I'LL THINK ABOUT IT...
AND NOW, IF YOU'LL EXCUSE ME, IT'S NOON...
HE SEEMS TO BE IN A HURRY...
HIS SACRO-SANCT 12:05 MEETING, MR. CASTERMAN! AT THE CARREFOUR GALLERY. HE GOES EVERY DAY. PAINTING AND MODERN ART ARE ALL HE THINKS ABOUT...
BEEP!
HOW CAN WE GET HIM BACK TO WORK, BOB?
BEATS ME!
GALERIE CARREFOUR
Rekord

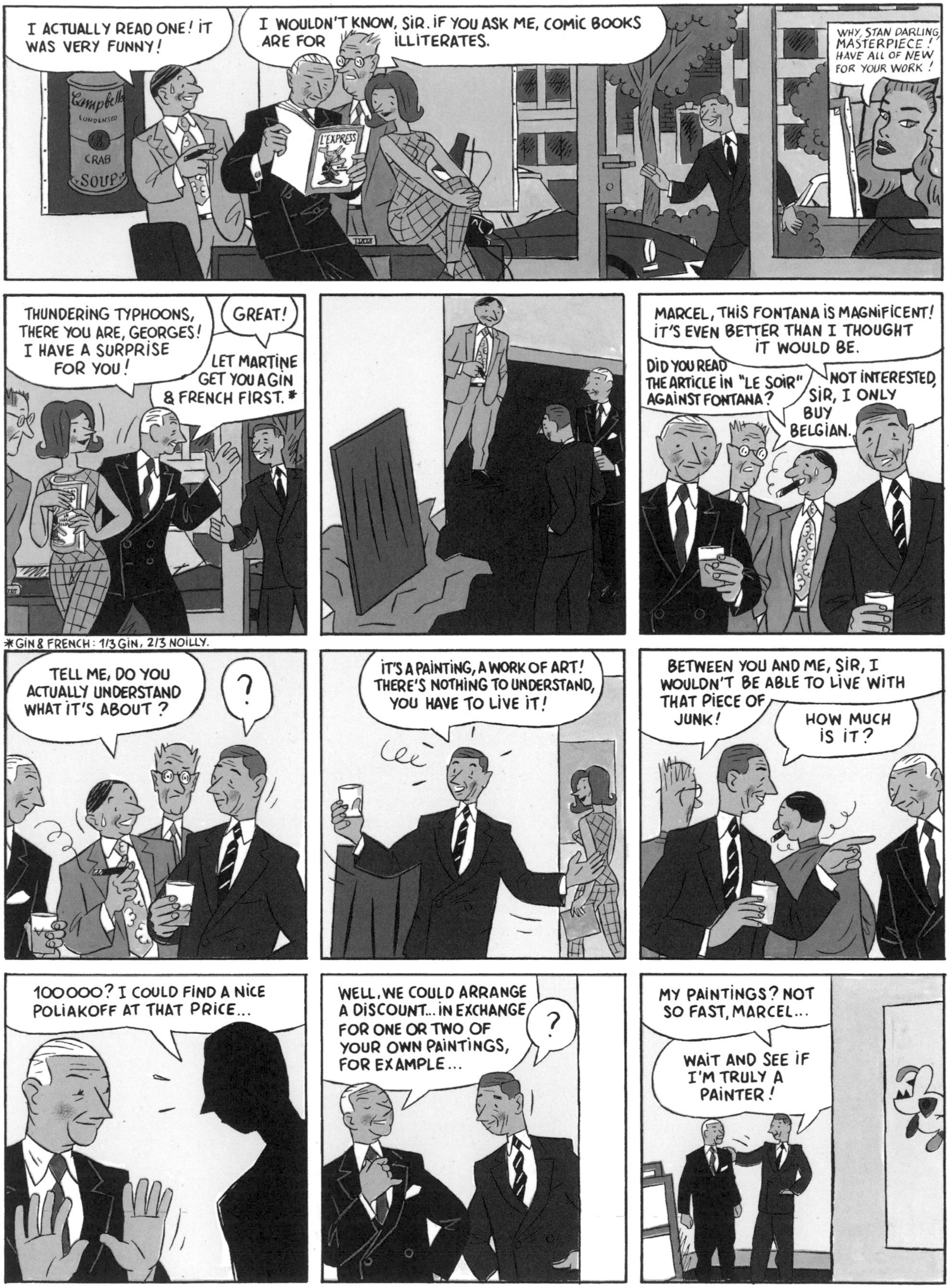
I ACTUALLY READ ONE! IT WAS VERY FUNNY!
I WOULDN'T KNOW, SIR. IF YOU ASK ME, COMIC BOOKS ARE FOR ILLITERATES.
L'EXPRESS
CRAB SOUP
WHY, STAN DARLING, MASTERPIECE! HAVE ALL OF NEW FOR YOUR WORK!
THUNDERING TYPHOONS, THERE YOU ARE, GEORGES! I HAVE A SURPRISE FOR YOU!
GREAT!
LET MARTINE GET YOU A GIN & FRENCH FIRST.*
MARCEL, THIS FONTANA IS MAGNIFICENT! IT'S EVEN BETTER THAN I THOUGHT IT WOULD BE.
DID YOU READ THE ARTICLE IN "LE SOIR" AGAINST FONTANA?
NOT INTERESTED, SIR, I ONLY BUY BELGIAN.
*GIN & FRENCH: 1/3 GIN, 2/3 NOILLY.
TELL ME, DO YOU ACTUALLY UNDERSTAND WHAT IT'S ABOUT?
?
IT'S A PAINTING, A WORK OF ART! THERE'S NOTHING TO UNDERSTAND, YOU HAVE TO LIVE IT!
BETWEEN YOU AND ME, SIR, I WOULDN'T BE ABLE TO LIVE WITH THAT PIECE OF JUNK!
HOW MUCH IS IT?
100 000? I COULD FIND A NICE POLIAKOFF AT THAT PRICE...
WELL, WE COULD ARRANGE A DISCOUNT... IN EXCHANGE FOR ONE OR TWO OF YOUR OWN PAINTINGS, FOR EXAMPLE...
?
MY PAINTINGS? NOT SO FAST, MARCEL...
WAIT AND SEE IF I'M TRULY A PAINTER!

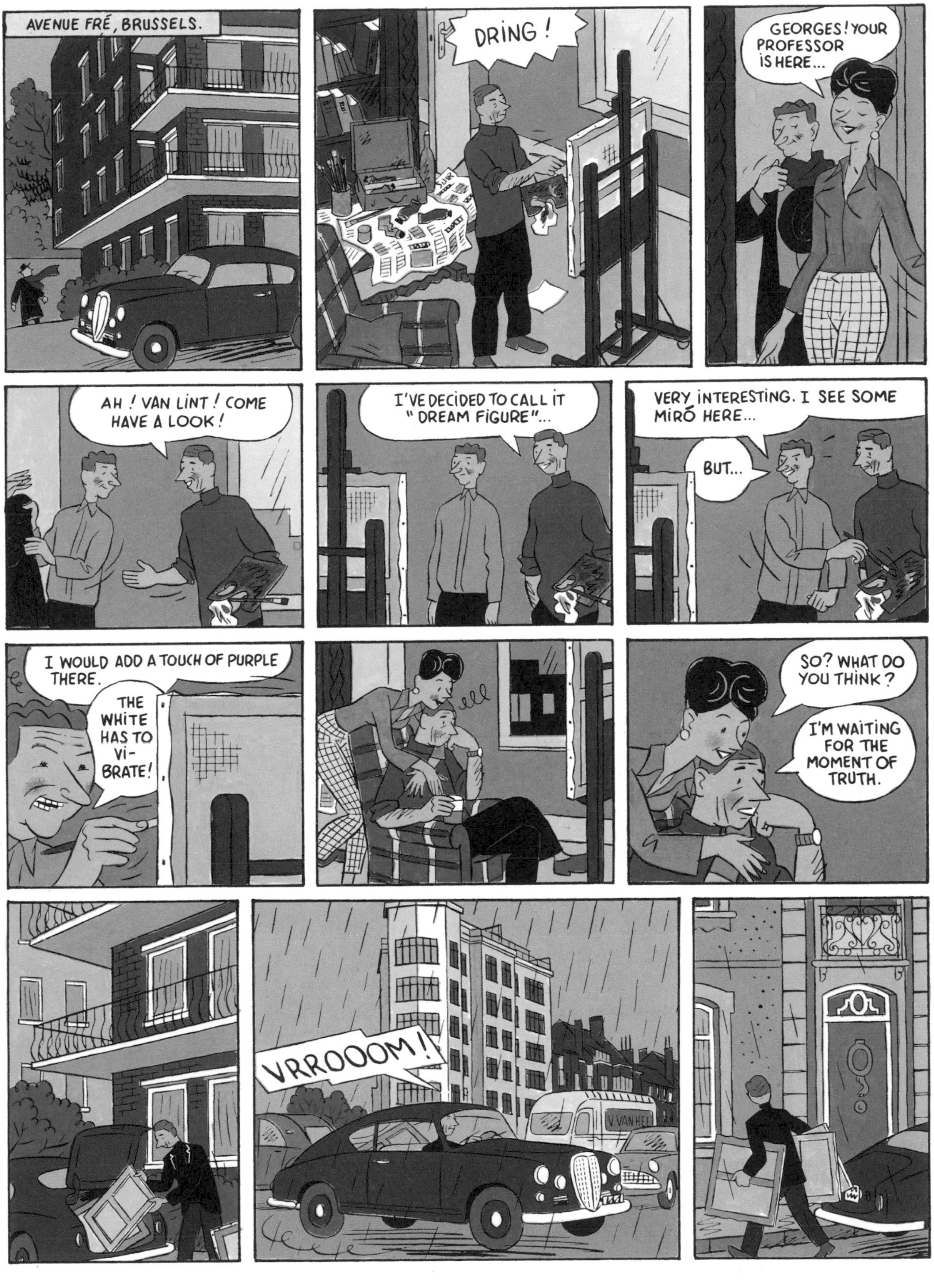
AVENUE FRÉ, BRUSSELS.
DRING!
GEORGES! YOUR PROFESSOR IS HERE...
AH! VAN LINT! COME HAVE A LOOK!
I'VE DECIDED TO CALL IT "DREAM FIGURE"...
VERY INTERESTING. I SEE SOME MIRÓ HERE...
BUT...
I WOULD ADD A TOUCH OF PURPLE THERE.
THE WHITE HAS TO VI-BRATE!
SO? WHAT DO YOU THINK?
I'M WAITING FOR THE MOMENT OF TRUTH.
VRROOOM!
V. VANHEE

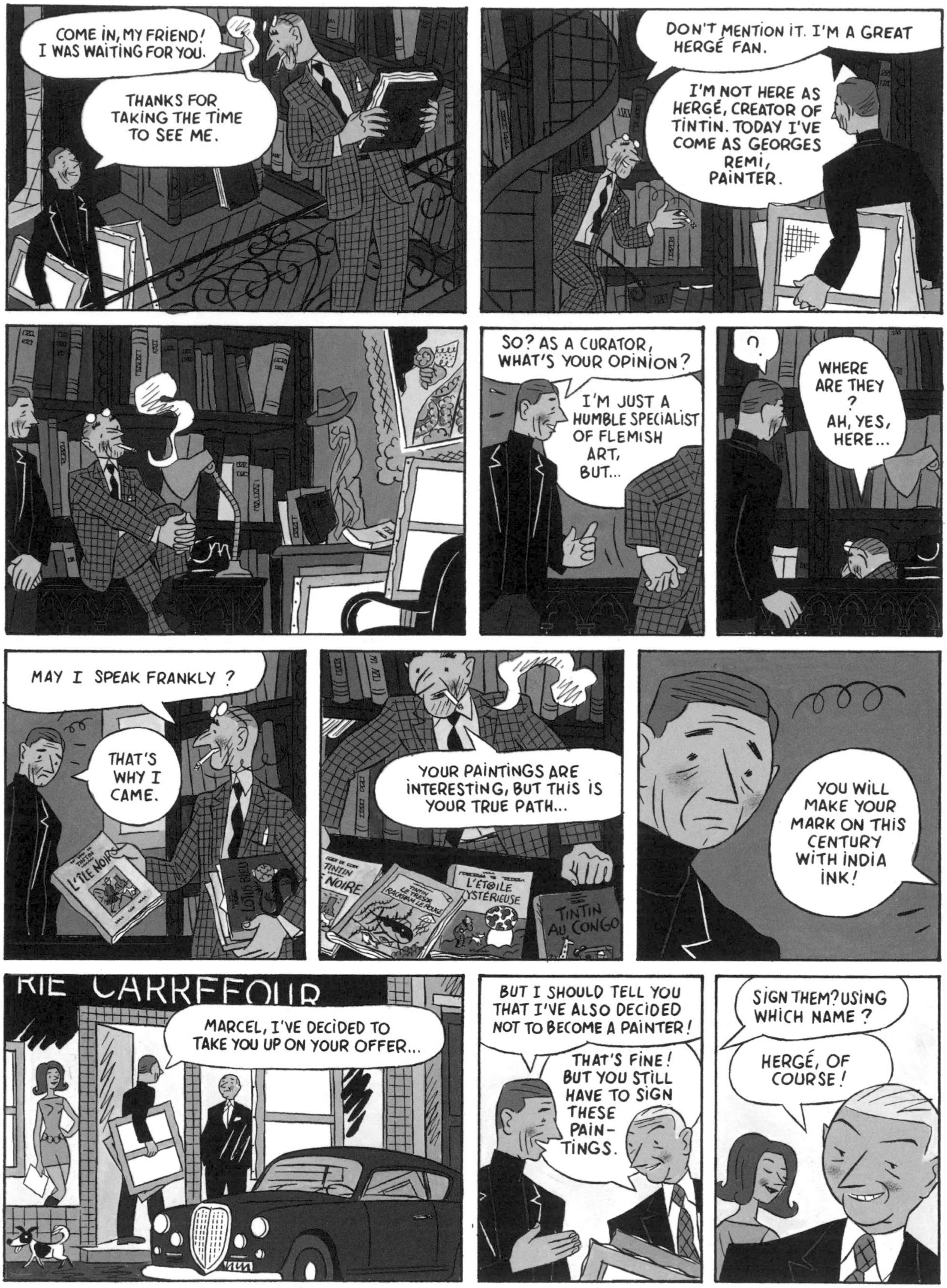
COME IN, MY FRIEND! I WAS WAITING FOR YOU.
THANKS FOR TAKING THE TIME TO SEE ME.
DON'T MENTION IT. I'M A GREAT HERGÉ FAN.
I'M NOT HERE AS HERGÉ, CREATOR OF TINTIN. TODAY I'VE COME AS GEORGES REMI, PAINTER.
SO? AS A CURATOR, WHAT'S YOUR OPINION?
I'M JUST A HUMBLE SPECIALIST OF FLEMISH ART, BUT...
?
WHERE ARE THEY ? AH, YES, HERE...
MAY I SPEAK FRANKLY ?
THAT'S WHY I CAME.
L'ILE NOIRE
LOTUS BLEU
YOUR PAINTINGS ARE INTERESTING, BUT THIS IS YOUR TRUE PATH...
TINTIN
L'ETOILE MYSTERIEUSE
TINTIN LE TRESOR DE RACKHAM LE ROUGE
TINTIN AU CONGO
YOU WILL MAKE YOUR MARK ON THIS CENTURY WITH INDIA INK!
RIE CARREFOUR
MARCEL, I'VE DECIDED TO TAKE YOU UP ON YOUR OFFER...
BUT I SHOULD TELL YOU THAT I'VE ALSO DECIDED NOT TO BECOME A PAINTER!
THAT'S FINE! BUT YOU STILL HAVE TO SIGN THESE PAIN-TINGS.
SIGN THEM? USING WHICH NAME ?
HERGÉ, OF COURSE!

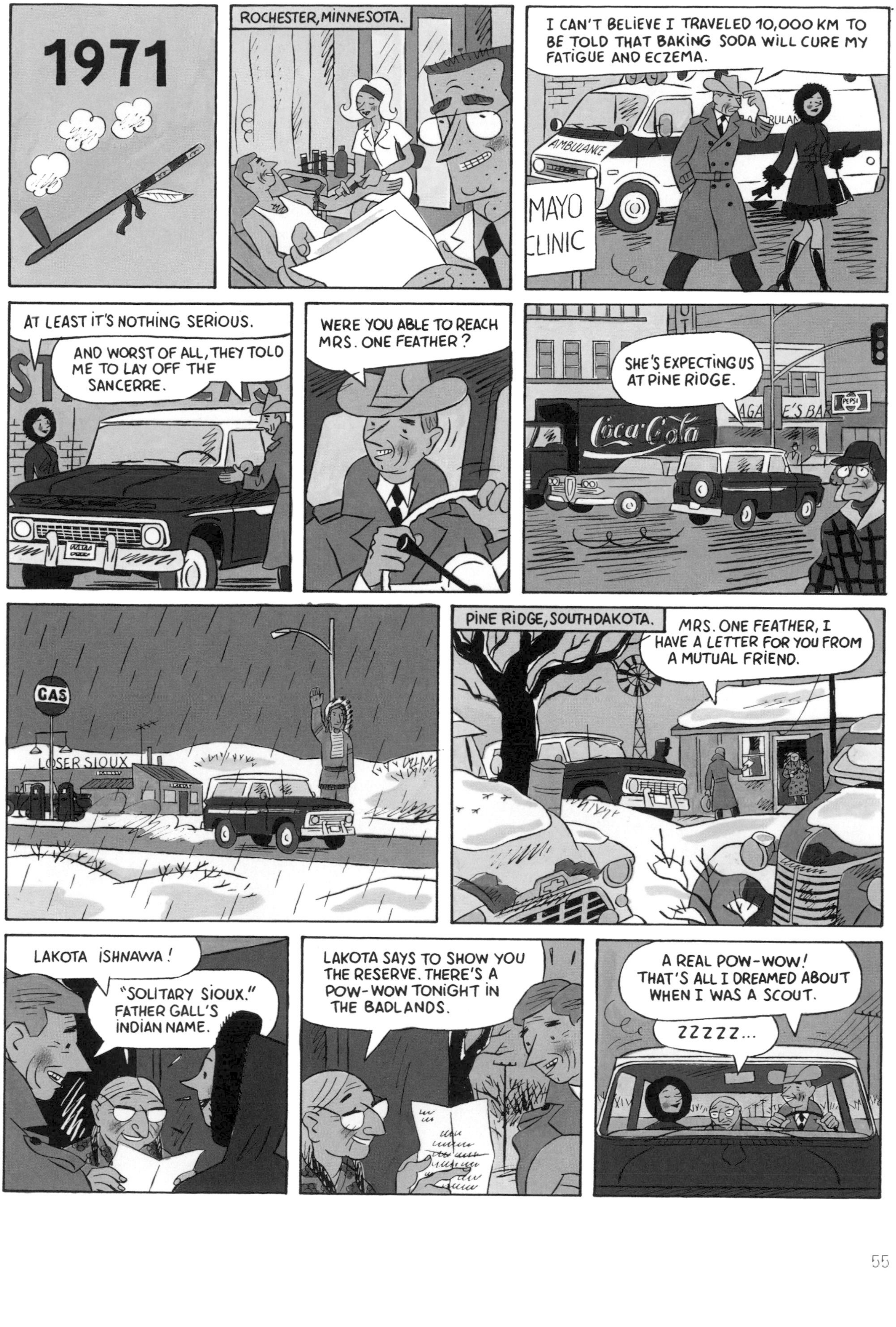

1971
ROCHESTER, MINNESOTA.
I CAN'T BELIEVE I TRAVELED 10,000 KM TO BE TOLD THAT BAKING SODA WILL CURE MY FATIGUE AND ECZEMA.
AMBULANCE
MAYO
CLINIC
AT LEAST IT'S NOTHING SERIOUS.
AND WORST OF ALL, THEY TOLD ME TO LAY OFF THE SANCERRE.
WERE YOU ABLE TO REACH MRS. ONE FEATHER?
SHE'S EXPECTING US AT PINE RIDGE.
Coca-Cola
PEPSI
GAS
LOSER SIOUX
PINE RIDGE, SOUTH DAKOTA.
MRS. ONE FEATHER, I HAVE A LETTER FOR YOU FROM A MUTUAL FRIEND.
LAKOTA ISHNAWA!
"SOLITARY SIOUX." FATHER GALL'S INDIAN NAME.
LAKOTA SAYS TO SHOW YOU THE RESERVE. THERE'S A POW-WOW TONIGHT IN THE BADLANDS.
A REAL POW-WOW! THAT'S ALL I DREAMED ABOUT WHEN I WAS A SCOUT.
ZZZZZ...

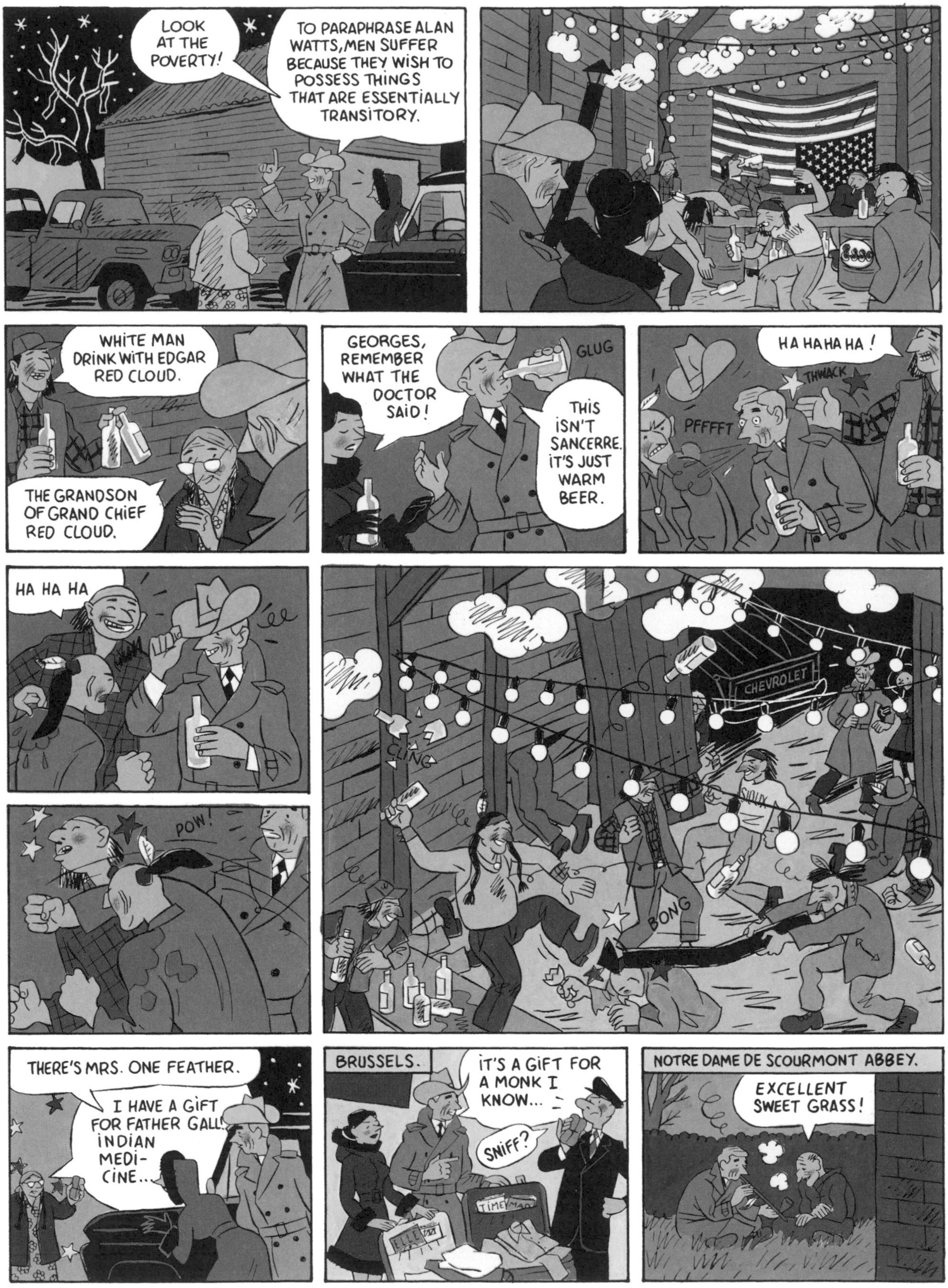
LOOK AT THE POVERTY!
TO PARAPHRASE ALAN WATTS, MEN SUFFER BECAUSE THEY WISH TO POSSESS THINGS THAT ARE ESSENTIALLY TRANSITORY.
ESSO
WHITE MAN DRINK WITH EDGAR RED CLOUD.
THE GRANDSON OF GRAND CHIEF RED CLOUD.
GEORGES, REMEMBER WHAT THE DOCTOR SAID!
GLUG
THIS ISN'T SANCERRE. IT'S JUST WARM BEER.
HA HA HA HA!
THWACK
PFFFFT
HA HA HA
POW!
CHEVROLET
CLING
SIOUX
BONG
THERE'S MRS. ONE FEATHER.
I HAVE A GIFT FOR FATHER GALL! INDIAN MEDICINE...
BRUSSELS.
IT'S A GIFT FOR A MONK I KNOW...
SNIFF?
TIME
ELLE
NOTRE DAME DE SCOURMONT ABBEY.
EXCELLENT SWEET GRASS!

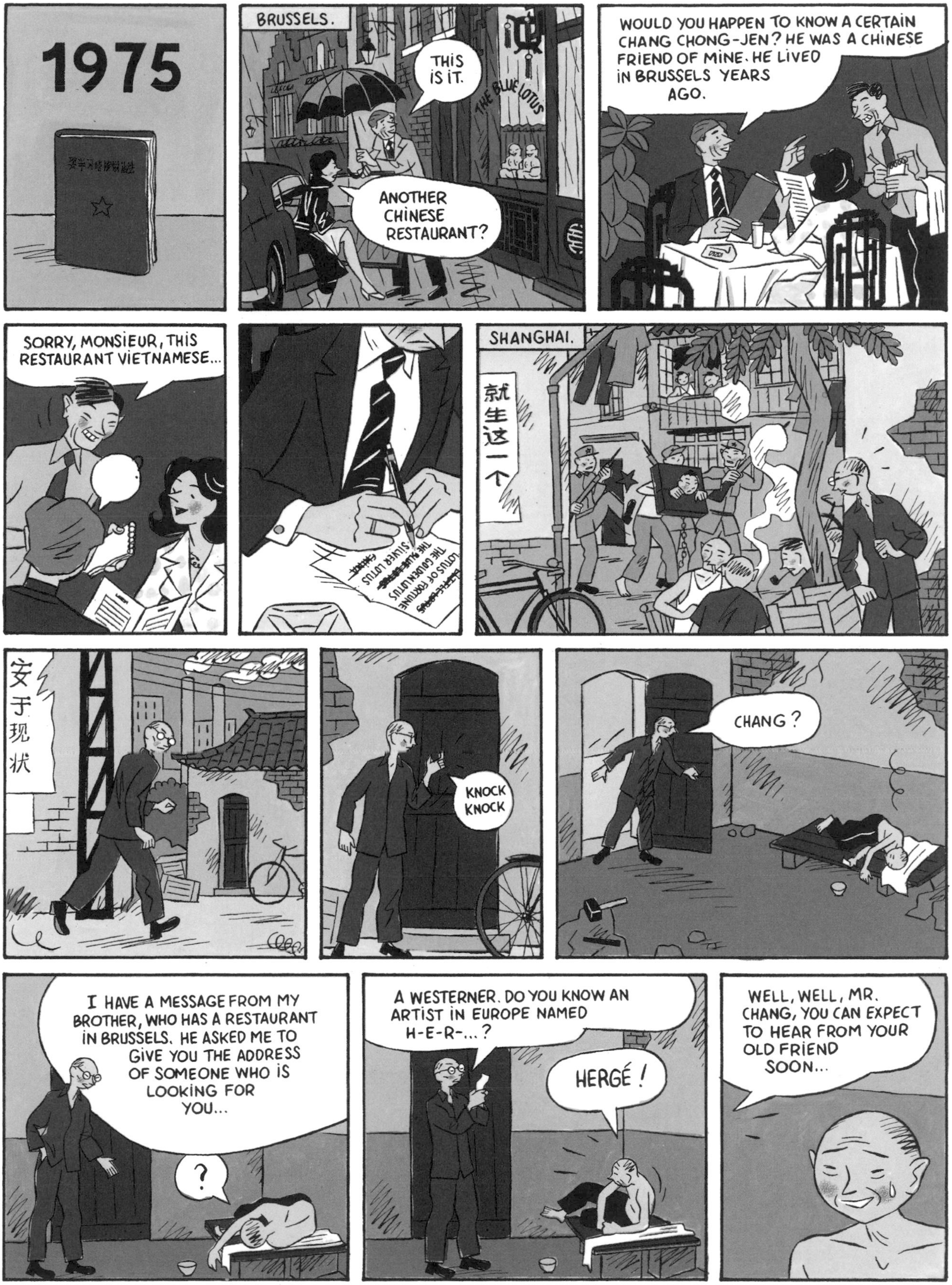
1975
BRUSSELS.
THIS IS IT.
THE BLUE LOTUS
ANOTHER CHINESE RESTAURANT?
WOULD YOU HAPPEN TO KNOW A CERTAIN CHANG CHONG-JEN? HE WAS A CHINESE FRIEND OF MINE. HE LIVED IN BRUSSELS YEARS AGO.
SORRY, MONSIEUR, THIS RESTAURANT VIETNAMESE...
THE GOLDEN LOTUS
SILVER LOTUS
SHANGHAI.
就生这一个
安于现状
KNOCK KNOCK
CHANG?
I HAVE A MESSAGE FROM MY BROTHER, WHO HAS A RESTAURANT IN BRUSSELS. HE ASKED ME TO GIVE YOU THE ADDRESS OF SOMEONE WHO IS LOOKING FOR YOU...
?
A WESTERNER. DO YOU KNOW AN ARTIST IN EUROPE NAMED H-E-R-...?
HERGÉ!
WELL, WELL, MR. CHANG, YOU CAN EXPECT TO HEAR FROM YOUR OLD FRIEND SOON...

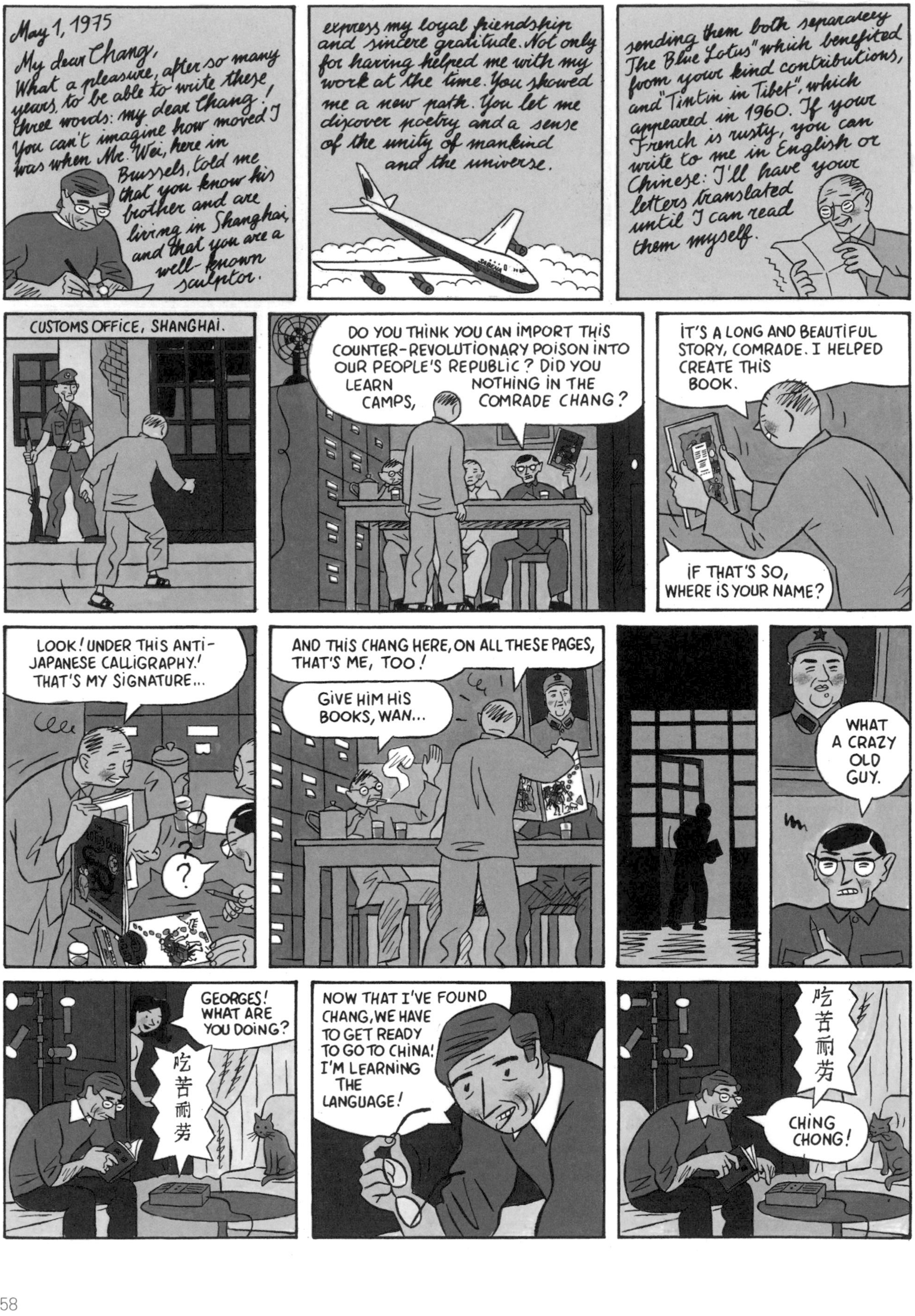
May 1, 1975
My dear Chang,
What a pleasure, after so many years, to be able to write these three words: my dear Chang! You can't imagine how moved I was when Mr. Wei, here in Brussels, told me that you know his brother and are living in Shanghai, and that you are a well-known sculptor.
express my loyal friendship and sincere gratitude. Not only for having helped me with my work at the time. You showed me a new path. You let me discover poetry and a sense of the unity of mankind and the universe.
sending them both separately The Blue Lotus" which benefited from your kind contributions, and "Tintin in Tibet", which appeared in 1960. If your French is rusty, you can write to me in English or Chinese: I'll have your letters translated until I can read them myself.
CUSTOMS OFFICE, SHANGHAI.
DO YOU THINK YOU CAN IMPORT THIS COUNTER-REVOLUTIONARY POISON INTO OUR PEOPLE'S REPUBLIC? DID YOU LEARN NOTHING IN THE CAMPS, COMRADE CHANG?
IT'S A LONG AND BEAUTIFUL STORY, COMRADE. I HELPED CREATE THIS BOOK.
IF THAT'S SO, WHERE IS YOUR NAME?
LOOK! UNDER THIS ANTI-JAPANESE CALLIGRAPHY! THAT'S MY SIGNATURE...
?
AND THIS CHANG HERE, ON ALL THESE PAGES, THAT'S ME, TOO!
GIVE HIM HIS BOOKS, WAN...
WHAT A CRAZY OLD GUY.
GEORGES! WHAT ARE YOU DOING?
吃苦耐劳
NOW THAT I'VE FOUND CHANG, WE HAVE TO GET READY TO GO TO CHINA! I'M LEARNING THE LANGUAGE!
吃苦耐劳
CHING CHONG!

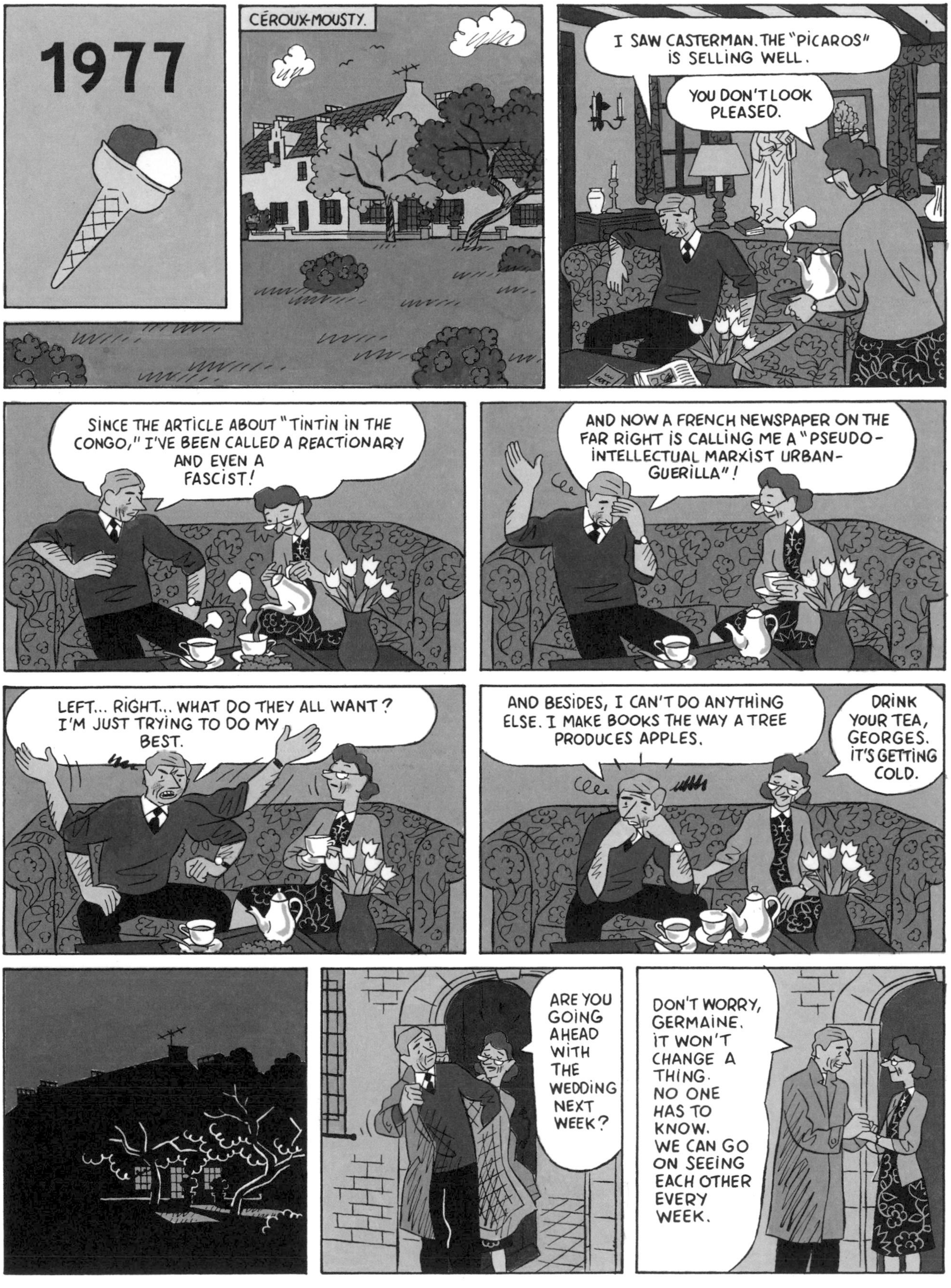
1977
CÉROUX-MOUSTY.
I SAW CASTERMAN. THE "PICAROS" IS SELLING WELL.
YOU DON'T LOOK PLEASED.
SINCE THE ARTICLE ABOUT "TINTIN IN THE CONGO," I'VE BEEN CALLED A REACTIONARY AND EVEN A FASCIST!
AND NOW A FRENCH NEWSPAPER ON THE FAR RIGHT IS CALLING ME A "PSEUDO-INTELLECTUAL MARXIST URBAN-GUERILLA"!
LEFT... RIGHT... WHAT DO THEY ALL WANT? I'M JUST TRYING TO DO MY BEST.
AND BESIDES, I CAN'T DO ANYTHING ELSE. I MAKE BOOKS THE WAY A TREE PRODUCES APPLES.
DRINK YOUR TEA, GEORGES. IT'S GETTING COLD.
ARE YOU GOING AHEAD WITH THE WEDDING NEXT WEEK?
DON'T WORRY, GERMAINE. IT WON'T CHANGE A THING. NO ONE HAS TO KNOW. WE CAN GO ON SEEING EACH OTHER EVERY WEEK.

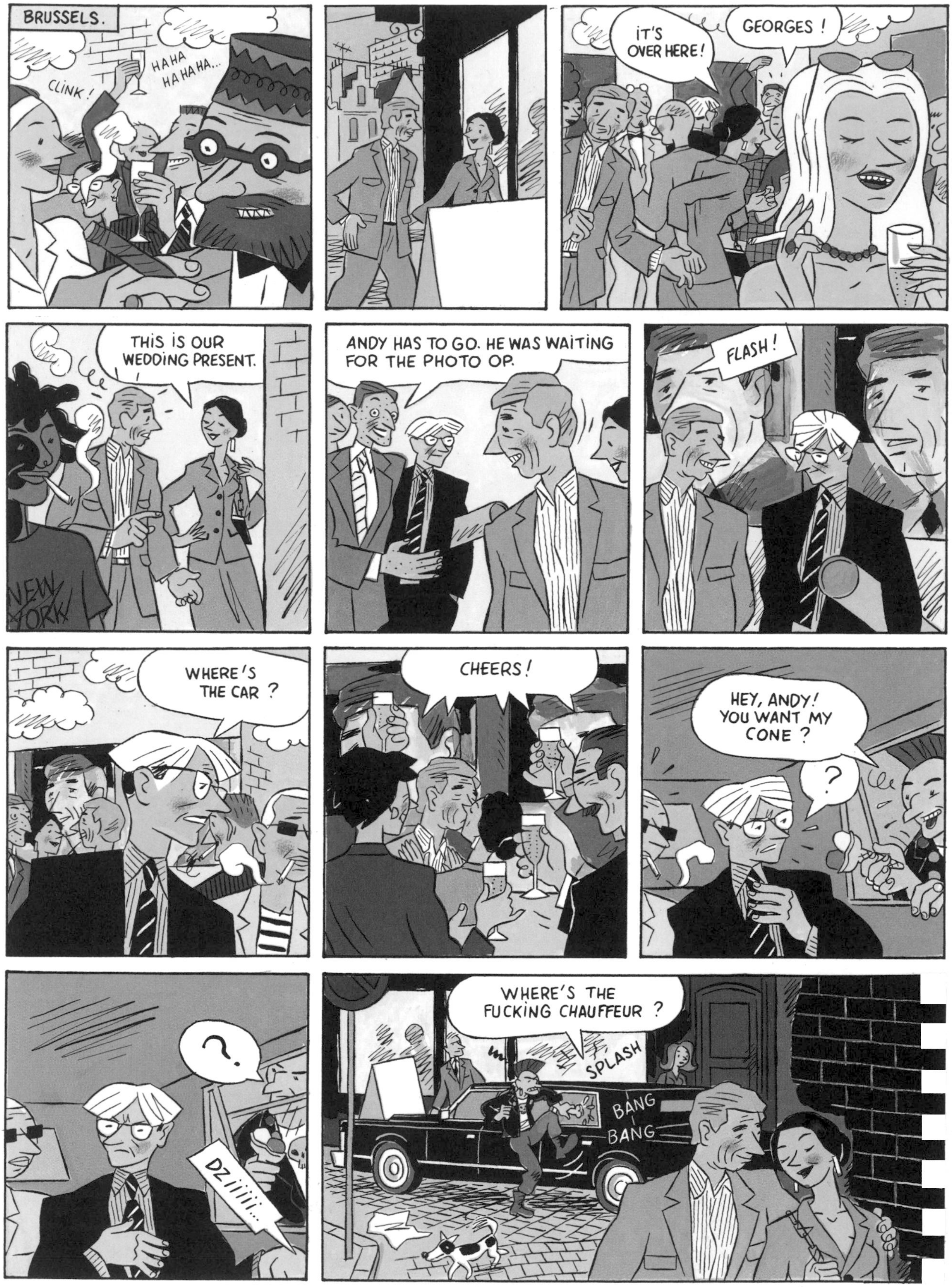
BRUSSELS.
CLINK!
HAHA HAHAHA...
IT'S OVER HERE!
GEORGES!
THIS IS OUR WEDDING PRESENT.
ANDY HAS TO GO. HE WAS WAITING FOR THE PHOTO OP.
FLASH!
NEW YORK
WHERE'S THE CAR ?
CHEERS!
HEY, ANDY! YOU WANT MY CONE ?
?
?
DZIIIII...
WHERE'S THE FUCKING CHAUFFEUR ?
SPLASH
BANG
BANG

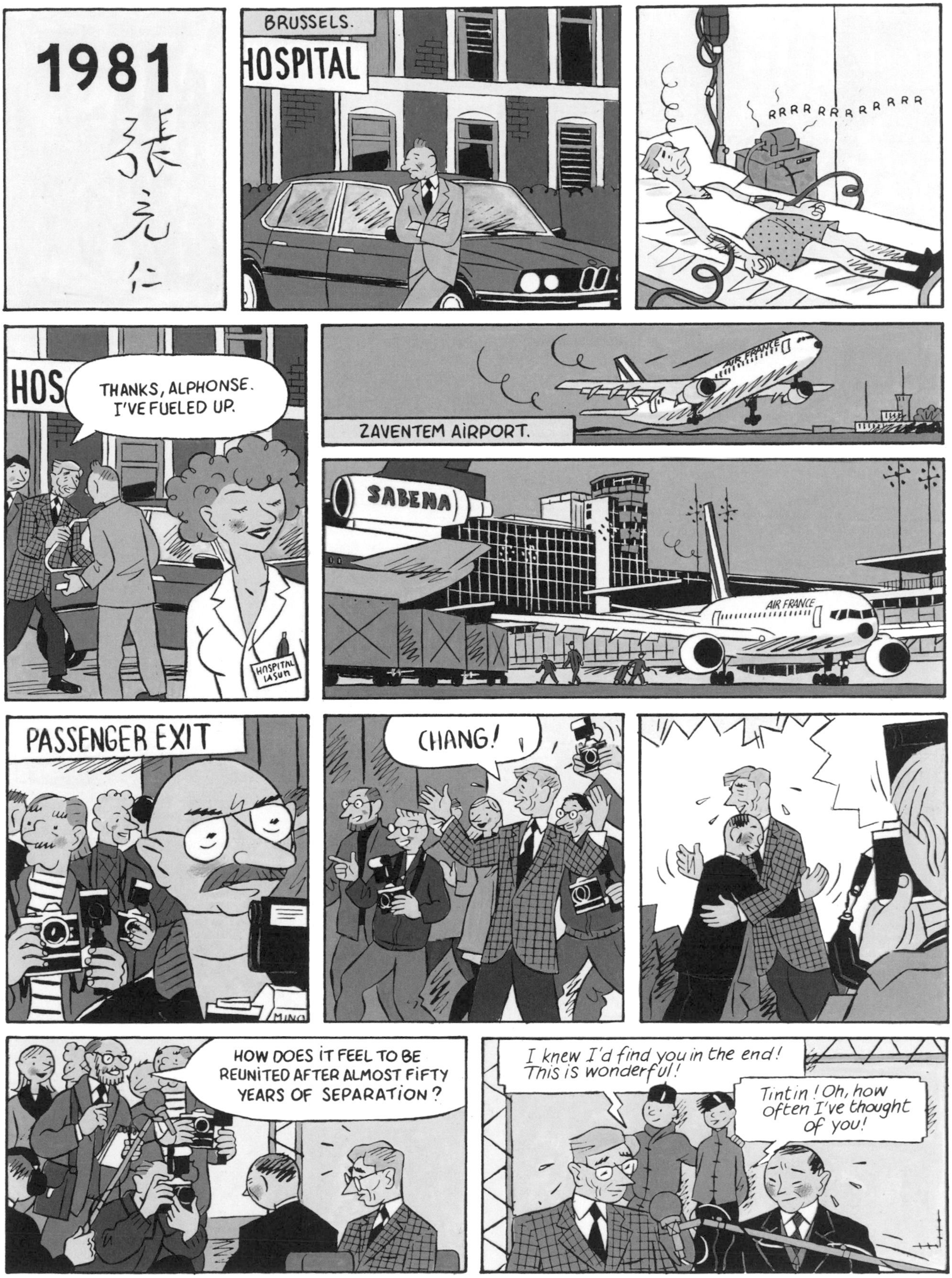
1981
張充仁
BRUSSELS.
HOSPITAL
RRRRRRRRRRRRR
HOS
THANKS, ALPHONSE. I'VE FUELED UP.
HOSPITAL
ZAVENTEM AIRPORT.
AIR FRANCE
SABENA
AIR FRANCE
PASSENGER EXIT
CHANG!
HOW DOES IT FEEL TO BE REUNITED AFTER ALMOST FIFTY YEARS OF SEPARATION?
I knew I'd find you in the end! This is wonderful!
Tintin! Oh, how often I've thought of you!

A PAINTER PAINTED FOUR FLOWERS — ONE YELLOW, ONE RED, ONE GREEN AND ONE WHITE...

HERGÉ STUDIO.

HE WAS ASKED TO FILL THE WHITE ONE WITH CALLIGRAPHY. HE REFUSED, SAYING: "WHITE IS WORTH MORE THAN GOLD, FIRE AND JADE..."

BECAUSE WHITE IS EMPTY, AND EMPTINESS IS PRECIOUS.

SORRY THAT I'M LATE.

HAS THE QUEEN ARRIVED?

SHE'S COMING!

CHANG CHONG-JEN.

YOU LOOK JUST LIKE YOU DO IN THE BOOKS.

PIERRE STERCKX.

FRANCE IS INTERESTED. YOUR APPLICATION FOR RESIDENCE IS COMING ALONG.

SO? WHEN CAN WE EXPECT A NEW TINTIN?

...

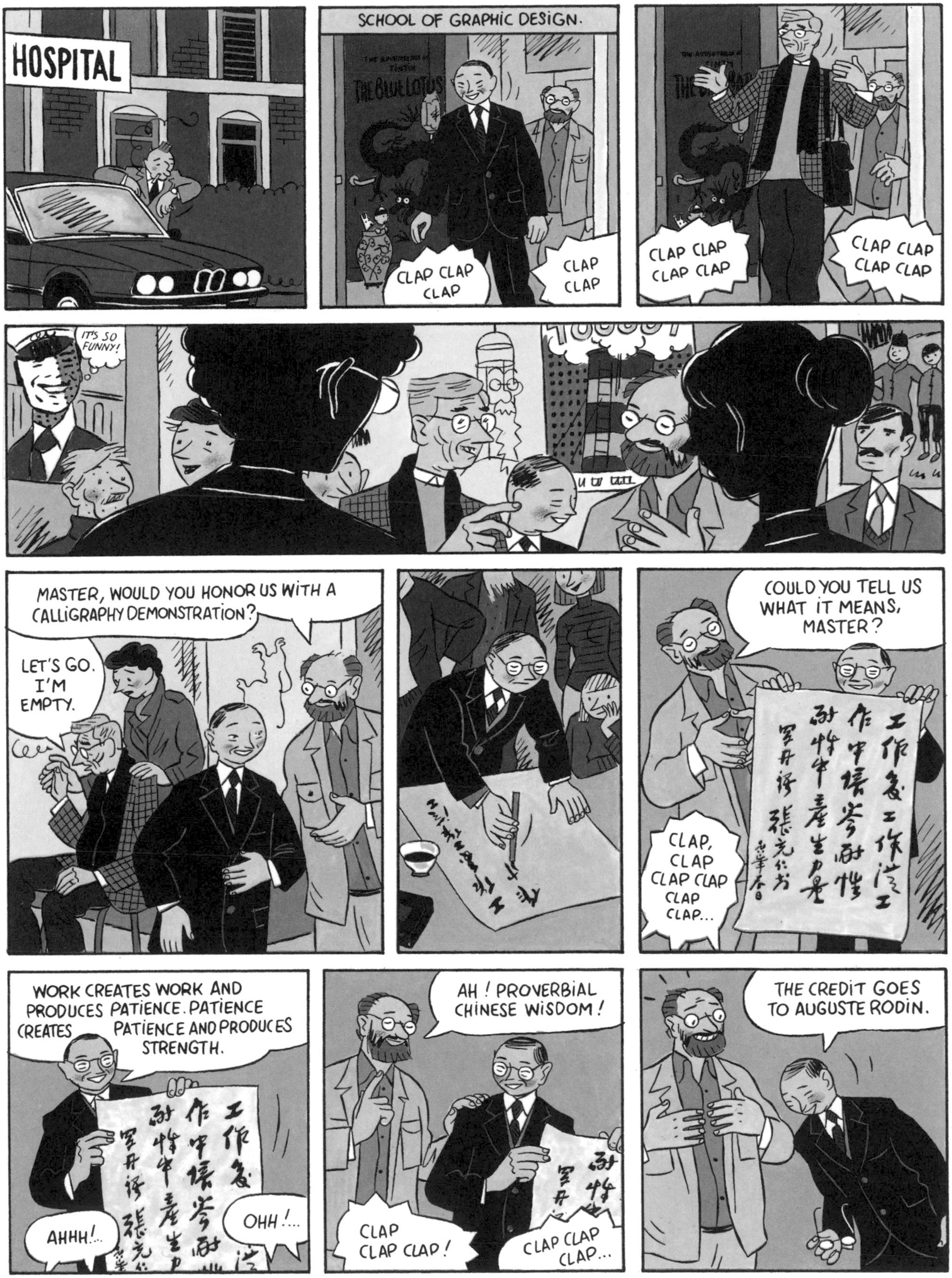
HOSPITAL
SCHOOL OF GRAPHIC DESIGN.
CLAP CLAP CLAP
CLAP CLAP
CLAP CLAP CLAP CLAP
CLAP CLAP CLAP CLAP
IT'S SO FUNNY!
MASTER, WOULD YOU HONOR US WITH A CALLIGRAPHY DEMONSTRATION?
LET'S GO. I'M EMPTY.
COULD YOU TELL US WHAT IT MEANS, MASTER?
CLAP, CLAP CLAP CLAP CLAP CLAP...
WORK CREATES WORK AND PRODUCES PATIENCE. PATIENCE CREATES PATIENCE AND PRODUCES STRENGTH.
AHHH!...
OHH!...
AH! PROVERBIAL CHINESE WISDOM!
CLAP CLAP CLAP!
CLAP CLAP CLAP...
THE CREDIT GOES TO AUGUSTE RODIN.

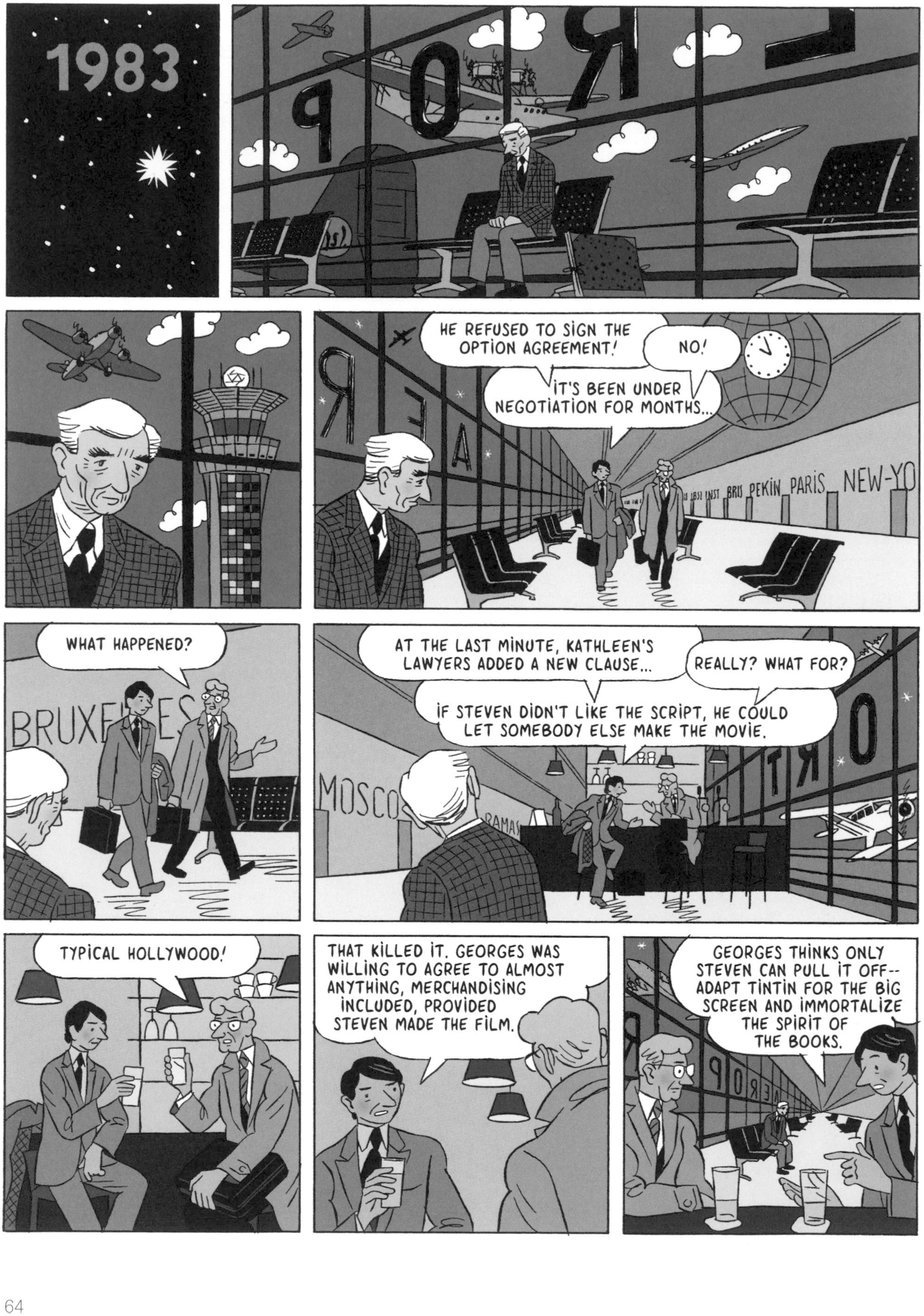
1983
HE REFUSED TO SIGN THE OPTION AGREEMENT!
NO!
IT'S BEEN UNDER NEGOTIATION FOR MONTHS...
PEKIN PARIS NEW-YO
WHAT HAPPENED?
BRUXE
AT THE LAST MINUTE, KATHLEEN'S LAWYERS ADDED A NEW CLAUSE...
REALLY? WHAT FOR?
IF STEVEN DIDN'T LIKE THE SCRIPT, HE COULD LET SOMEBODY ELSE MAKE THE MOVIE.
MOSCO
TYPICAL HOLLYWOOD!
THAT KILLED IT. GEORGES WAS WILLING TO AGREE TO ALMOST ANYTHING, MERCHANDISING INCLUDED, PROVIDED STEVEN MADE THE FILM.
GEORGES THINKS ONLY STEVEN CAN PULL IT OFF-- ADAPT TINTIN FOR THE BIG SCREEN AND IMMORTALIZE THE SPIRIT OF THE BOOKS.

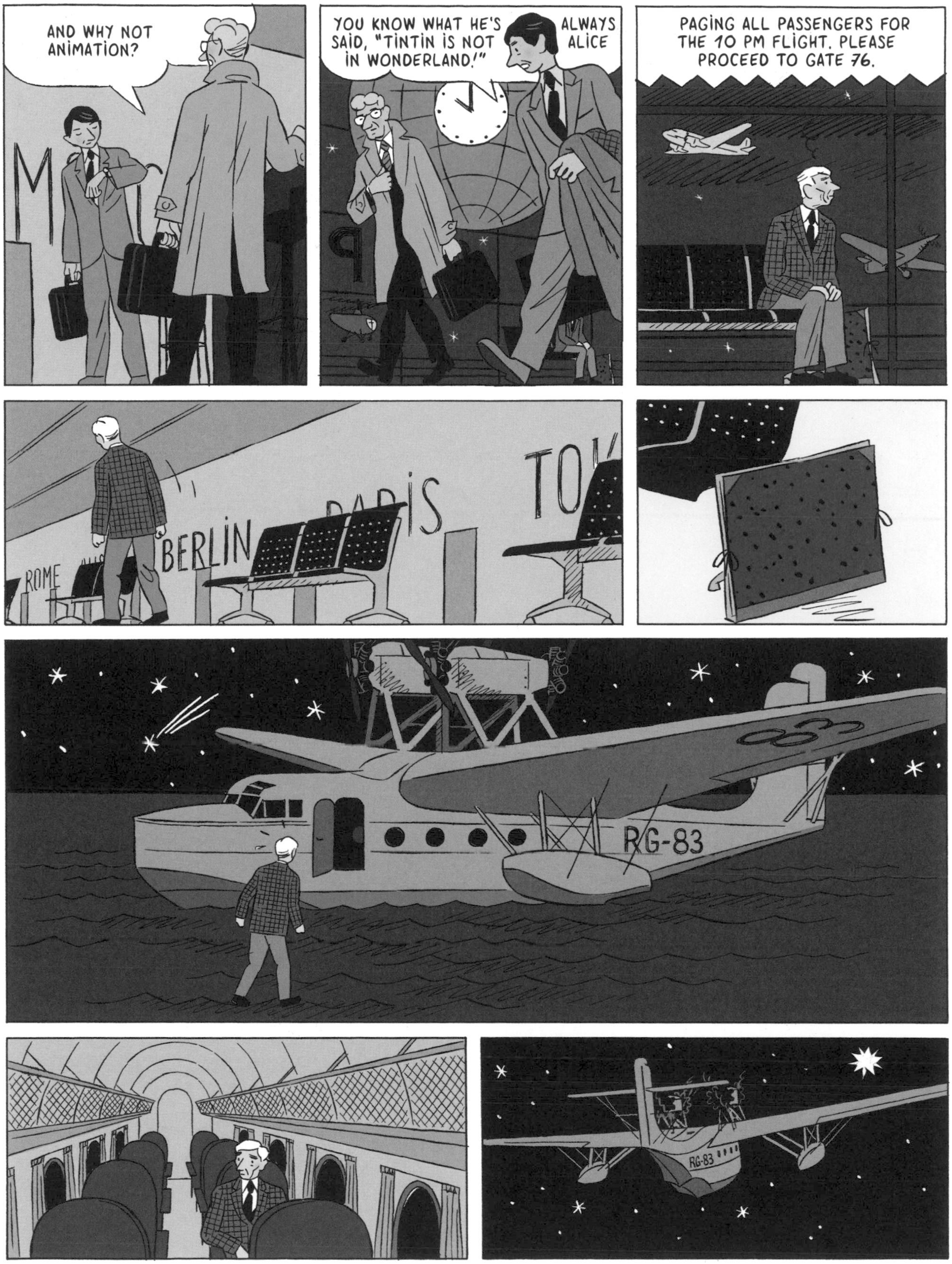
AND WHY NOT ANIMATION?
YOU KNOW WHAT HE'S ALWAYS SAID, "TINTIN IS NOT ALICE IN WONDERLAND!"
PAGING ALL PASSENGERS FOR THE 10 PM FLIGHT. PLEASE PROCEED TO GATE 76.
ROME
BERLIN
PARIS
RG-83
RG-83

BRUSSELS OBSERVATORY.

LOOK BETWEEN MARS AND JUPITER. YOU'LL SEE...

ASTEROID 1652, THE HERGÉ STAR!

YIKES!

?

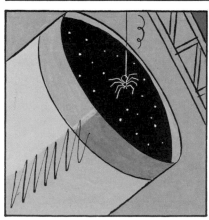

LE SOIR

LE SOIR

Elections in France and Germany: what's at stake.

The world bids fare-well to Hergé

The P believe against a

FIN

66

INDEX

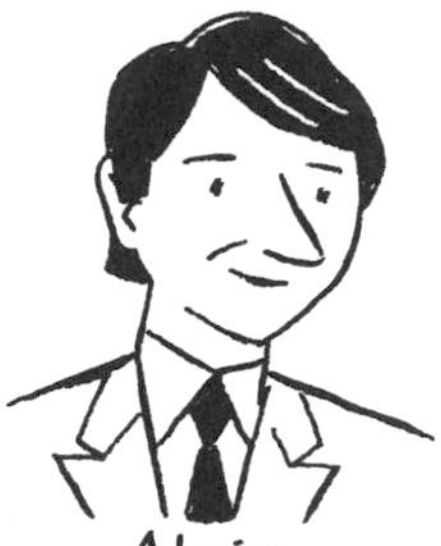

Alain
Baran.

A former ballet dancer born to a good family, this young Belgian became Georges's secretary in 1978. When the artist died, Baran created Varon International Licensing and Tintin Licensing, which managed the merchandising of the comic-book character and over which Georges's widow, Fanny Vlamynck, had no control. During the 1990s, a series of television cartoons proved to be a gold mine for Tintin Licensing. In the meantime, however, Baran had transferred the company, which was swallowed up by Canal Plus. In 1994, Fanny Vlamynck recovered the rights to Tintin.

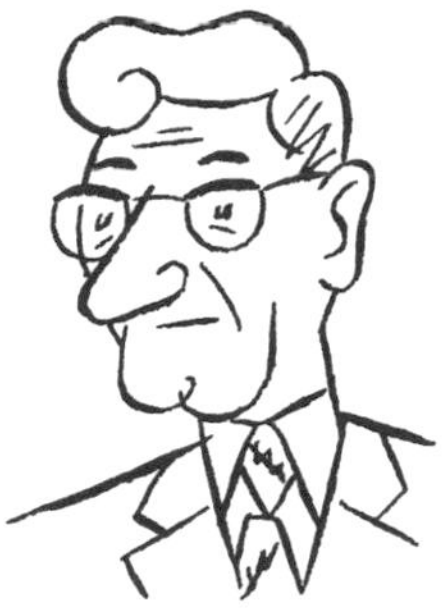

Louis-Robert
Casterman.

In 1945, twenty-five-year-old Louis-Robert succeeded his father, Louis-Henri, as the head of the family business, which was founded in 1780 by Donat-Joseph Casterman, a bookseller and editor from Tournai. In 1932, Charles Lesne, previously a journalist at the *XXe Siècle*, introduced Georges to the distinguished publishing house, which offered to take over the management of The Adventures of Tintin from the *Petit XXe*. The Tournai company published *The Blue Lotus* in 1936, but it wasn't until 1942 and *The Shooting Star* that Georges, prompted by his publisher, made his transition to color and the definitive 62-page format. After the war, Louis-Robert Casterman kept a close eye on every step of his star author's rise to fame. He died in 1994.

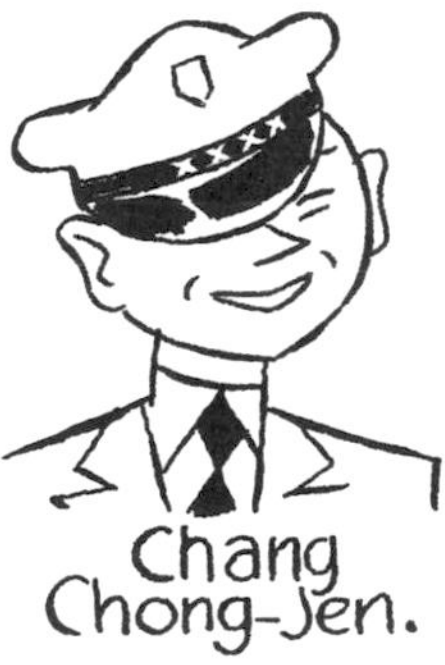

Chang
Chong-Jen.

Born on September 27, 1907 in Shanghai, this Chinese student came to Brussels to study at the Académie des Beaux-Arts in 1932. Father Gosset introduced him to Georges, who, a stickler for details, was doing research for his book *The Blue Lotus*. A strong friendship developed between the two young men, with Chang counseling Georges in the Chinese tradition of pen and ink drawing. In what seemed a natural development, he became one of the central characters in the *Lotus*. He left Brussels in 1935. Twenty-four years later, he reappeared in *Tintin in Tibet*—a premonition of actual events. After having lost sight of one another for almost fifty years, the two friends were reunited in 1981, following an endless paper chase by Georges to find Chang and bring him out of China, where he had suffered the brutality of the Cultural Revolution. Their highly publicized reunion culminated with Chang's triumphant tour of France and Belgium two years prior to Georges's death. Chang became a French citizen in 1989. He died in 1998.

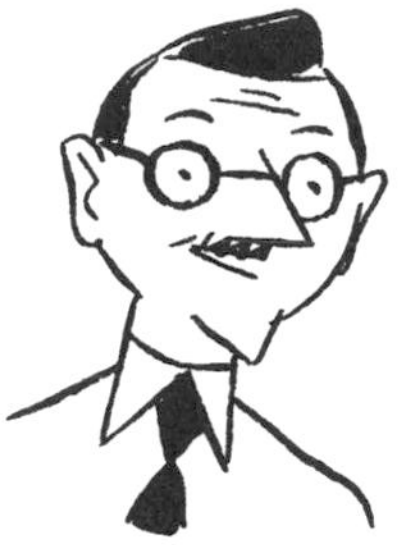

Bob
De Moor.

In 1945, Bob de Moor appeared on the scene as one of the promising new talents in Flemish comics. But his meeting with Georges in 1950 changed the course of his career. Involved in reworking some of the old books and drawing backgrounds for the new adventures, he quickly became the master's right-hand man. In charge of supervising the studio's advertisements and Tintin products, De Moor also faithfully contributed to the television cartoons and feature-length films. Additionally, the former prodigy drafted a solo project and published his own stories in *Le Journal de Tintin*. He was equally at ease with historical realism, *Cori le Mousaillon*, as he was with humor and clear line, *Barelli*. He died in 1992 without having achieved the dream of his career, to draw the last Tintin adventure, *L'Alph-art*.

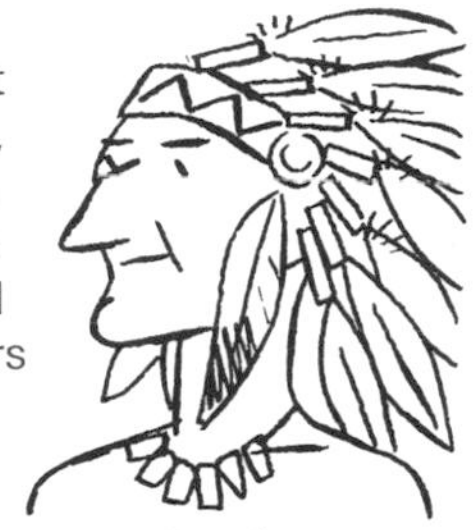

Gall

A Cistercian monk from Scourmont Abbey at Forges-les-Chimay, Belgium, Gall met Georges in the 1950s, when the artist, showing the first signs of chronic depression, came to find peace and meditate among members of the monastic orders. An authority on Native American culture, adopted by a Sioux tribe under the name Lakota Ishnawa, Father Gall's accounts fascinated Georges and no doubt contributed to his ever-increasing interest in ancient cultures and religions. As Georges's source of information about native culture, Gall contributed to *Les Peaux Rouges* (*The Red Skins*), one of the many Tintin projects that would ultimately be abandoned.

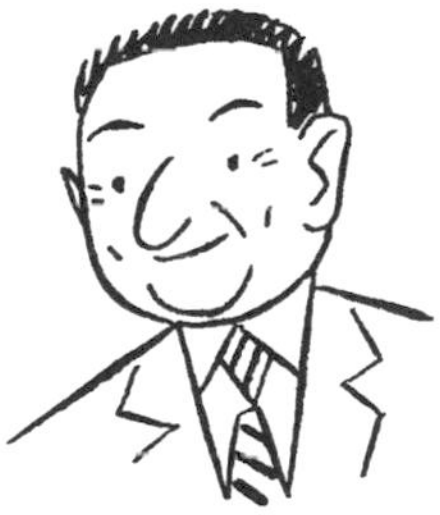

René
Goscinny.

The French scriptwriter made his debut in *Le Journal de Tintin* in 1956 with *Modeste et Pompom*, drawn by Franquin. Although he teamed up with many of the magazine's artists, Goscinny had little contact with Georges. Ten years later, the commercial triumph of Goscinny and Uderzo's Asterix would prompt Georges to take up painting. Charles de Gaulle once said that his only true rival was Tintin. For his part, the Belgian reporter's rival would always be Asterix.

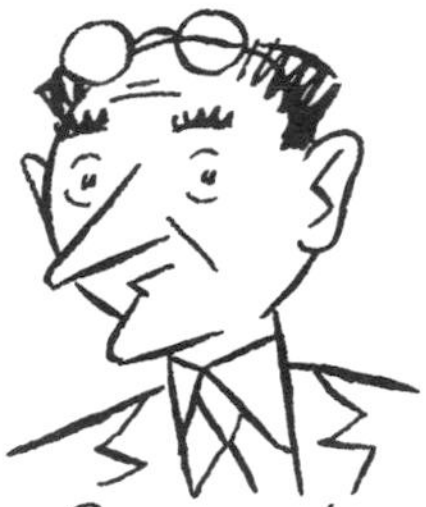

Bernard
Heuvelmans.

Successful author and a friend of Georges, this erudite Belgian invented a branch of science, cryptozoology, the study of mythical animals. *Destination Moon* and *Tintin in Tibet* benefited from Bernard's insightful advice.

A lover of music and art, Jacobs devoted himself to both disciplines from an early age. He made his debut at the Théâtre Royale de

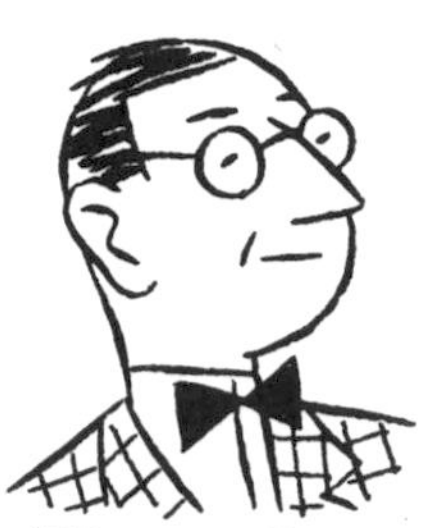

Edgar-Pierre Jacobs.

la Monnaie in Brussels in 1921, and went on to perform alongside Mistinguett at the Casino de Paris. His engagement with the Opéra de Lille marked the high point of his singing career. The events of 1940 put an end to his dreams, and Jacobs turned to illustration. In 1942, he took over the Flash Gordon series when Alex Raymond's original episodes were blocked in the United States. In the same year, Jacques Van Melkebeke, a childhood friend, introduced him to Georges. Although Jacobs had never read Tintin, he began working with Georges in 1944 when Georges decided to recast his black and white albums in color. Jacobs did the colors and backgrounds for *Tintin in America*, *King Ottokar's Scepter*, and *The Blue Lotus*. He was also a close collaborator in the creation of *Red Rackham's Treasure*, *The Seven Crystal Balls*, and *Prisoners of the Sun*. After the liberation, the two men undertook an unsuccessful joint effort under the pseudonym Olav. Jacobs moved on to do his own work for *Le Journal de Tintin*, launching the first story in the Blake and Mortimer series, *The Secret of the Swordfish*. A year later, he left Hergé's studio to embark on a dynamic solo career.

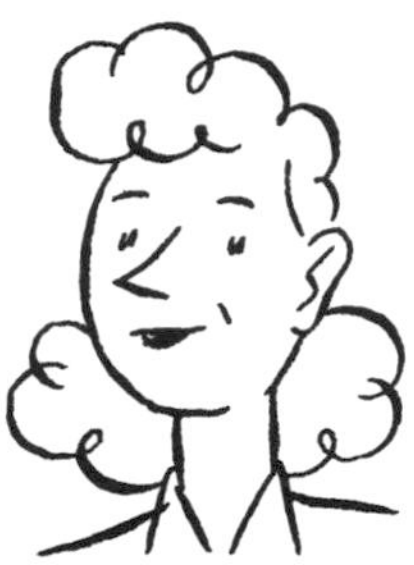

Germaine Kieckens.

Born in 1906, she was the secretary of Father Wallez, editor of the *XXe Siècle*. In a campaign to encourage employees to wed, Father Wallez played matchmaker to Kieckens and Georges. The energetic redhead attracted the enterprising young man, and Father Wallez presided over their wedding on July 21, 1932. Working with her husband, Germaine played a key role in developing Georges's career. Their relationship, which remained childless, seemed exceptionally solid until the early 1950s. Eventually, however, a rift developed between Georges and Germaine, who failed to take Tintin's overwhelming success seriously. In 1956, Georges began an affair with Fanny Vlamynck. Four years passed before he left Germaine, and another seventeen before he obtained a divorce. Until the end of his days, Georges returned to their villa in Céroux-Mousty every week to visit the woman who, having accompanied him in his career from the start, would always be considered the "Hergée" behind Hergé.

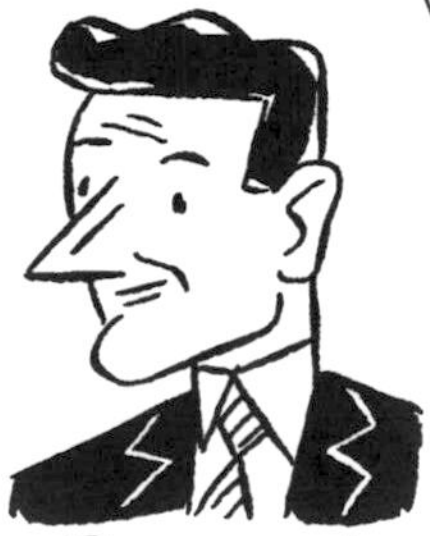

Raymond Leblanc.

After the liberation, Georges found himself in a delicate position: the new authorities refused to grant him the certificate of citizenship he needed to continue his career. Enter Raymond Leblanc. This hero of the Belgian resistance had ambitions: he wanted to create a magazine, *Le Journal de Tintin*. He also had paper and connections. In 1946, the weekly publication was launched. Named artistic director, Georges invited Jacobs, Martin, Cuvelier, and Van Melkebeke to his side, artists who would become the foundation of the Editions du Lombard. With this company, the entrepreneurial Leblanc began publishing comic albums in 1947, quickly taking over a large segment of the market, which he would continue to dominate for the next three decades.

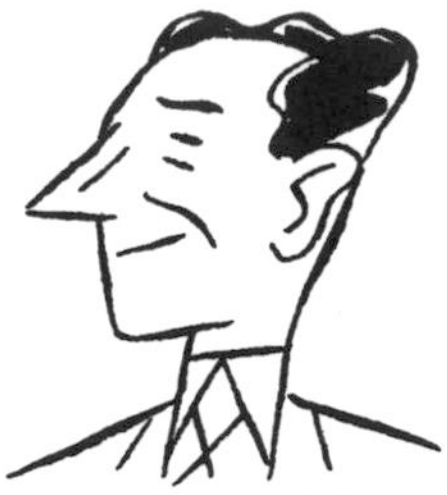

Léopold III.

On May 28, 1940, the King of Belgium surrendered to the German invaders. This decision launched a controversy that persists to this day. His marriage to a woman of low social standing in 1941, in the intimacy of the Chateau de Laeken, did not help matters. Georges, who sent signed copies of his books to the king and remained loyal to him at all times, was a regular guest at the de Laeken hunting parties.

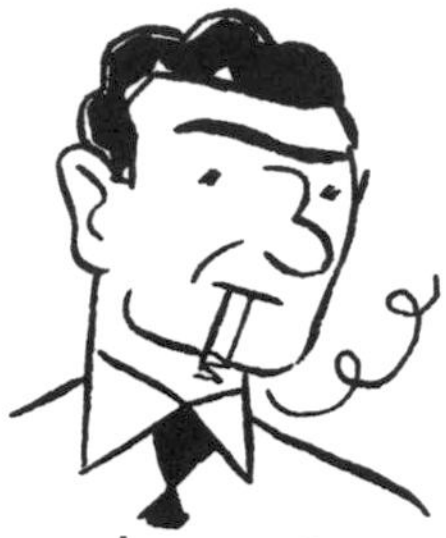

Jacques Martin.

This Frenchman, born in Strasbourg, drew his first sketches in the Messerschmitt factory in Augsburg, where the tides of war brought him in 1943. After using a pen name for several years, Jacques Martin launched the Alix series in *Le Journal de Tintin* in 1948, signing it with his own name. In 1952, he turned to contemporary adventure stories with Lefranc. Jacques joined the Hergé studio in 1953 and left in 1972, nineteen years later. He worked on all Tintin books produced during this period, taking credit for the "sticking-plaster" gag in *The Calculus Affair*. In the 1960s, he and Bob De Moor drew a Tintin page that sparked Georges's interest, but the matter was never followed up. No one other than Georges would ever draw Tintin.

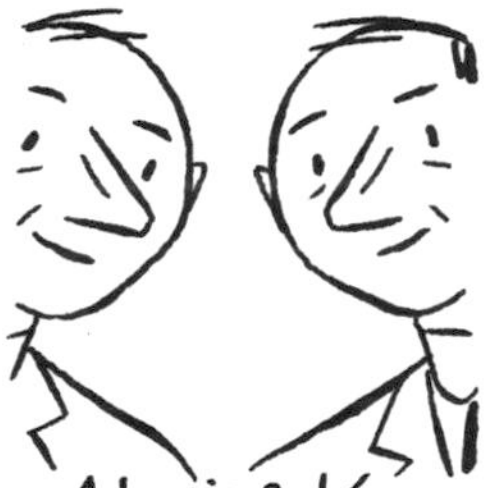

Alexis & Léon Remi.

Sons of Marie Dewigne and an unknown father, the twins Alexis and Léon Remi were born on October 1, 1882. They were raised "like family" by the Comtesse Errembault de Dudzeele at the Chaumont-Gistoux castle, where their mother worked as a maid. In 1892, Philippe Eugène Remi, a printer, married Marie and acknowledged her children. These unusual circumstances, possibly linking his father and uncle to aristocratic or even royal blood, were the source of a family secret that haunted Georges throughout his life. A moderate Catholic, Alexis was persuaded by Henri Van Roye-Waucqez, the owner of the clothing store where he worked as a clerk, to withdraw Georges from the "godless school" and enroll him in Saint-Boniface, where the boy's two vocations, scouting and drawing, blossomed. Although long overwhelmed by his son's ambitions, Alexis watched over his career throughout his life and in 1950, became manager of the Hergé studios. He and his identical twin, Léon, were a source of inspiration for the detectives Dupond and Dupont, known in English as Thompson and Thomson.

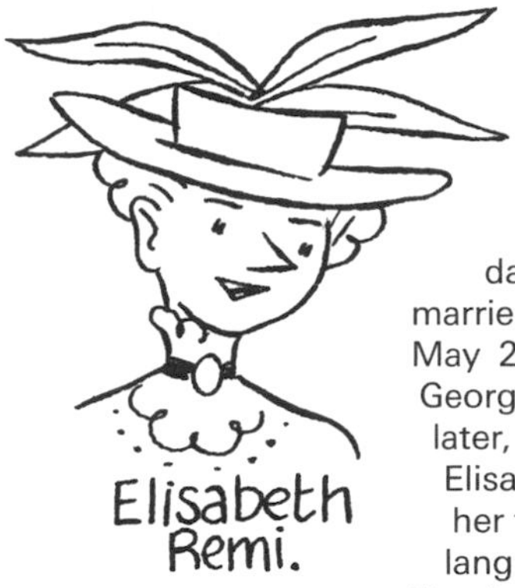
Elisabeth Remi.

Born in Brussels on February 20, 1882, Elisabeth Dufour, of Flemish origin and the daughter of a plumber-roofer, married Alexis Remi in 1905. On May 22, 1907, she gave birth to Georges Prosper Remi. Five years later, her son Paul was born. Elisabeth Remi was very close to her first son. She taught him her language (mother and son spoke Flemish when they were alone together) and shared with him her love for the big screen, taking young Georges to the movies every week. She died in 1946 in a psychiatric institution.

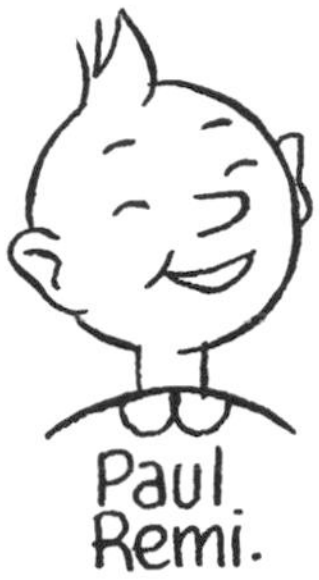
Paul Remi.

Born on March 26, 1912, Georges's younger brother chose a career in the army. He spent the war in an officer's internment camp in Germany. Escaping after several attempts to a Belgian unit in England, Major Remi returned to Brussels crowned with glory. In the early 1950s, Georges, who considered Paul irresponsible, offered unsuccessfully to adopt his two nephews. Paul, inclined to use the salty language of his fellow soldiers, was apparently a source of inspiration for Captain Haddock.

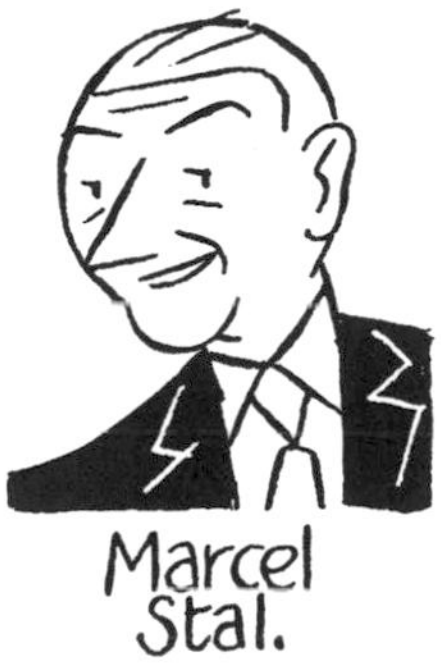
Marcel Stal.

Having befriended Georges through his brother Paul, whom he met in 1935 in artillery school, Marcel Stal left the army in 1960 with the rank of colonel. An art lover, he opened the Galerie Carrefour, to which Georges contributed the first three months of rent and which became the headquarters of Georges's life as an art enthusiast. Stal helped him build his collection. For many years, the gallery owner kept in his private possession two of the thirty-seven canvases produced by Georges during his brief career as a painter.

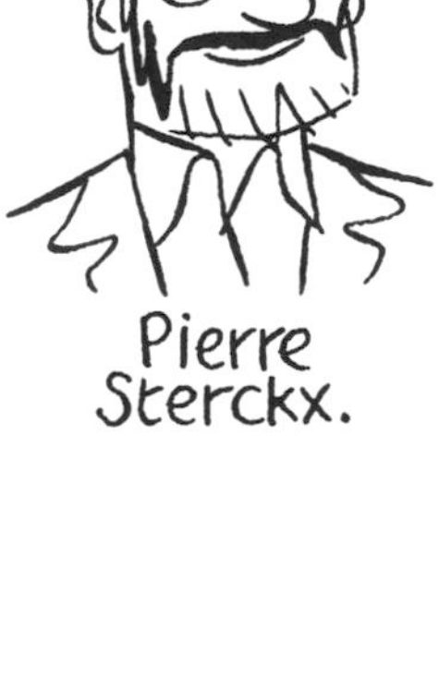
Pierre Sterckx.

Art critic and director of the design institute Ecole de Recherche Graphique in Brussels, he met Georges at the Galerie Carrefour in the 1960s. Eager to learn more about painting, Georges asked Sterckx to tutor him (the painter Van Lint would play a similar role with respect to pictorial technique). In 1979, Sterckx created the Musée Imaginaire de Tintin. Organizer of the 1981 exhibit "The Return of Chang," he was one of the discreet masterminds who coordinated the reunion of Georges and Chang. The first biography of Hergé was written by Sterckx, in collaboration with Thierry Smolderen.

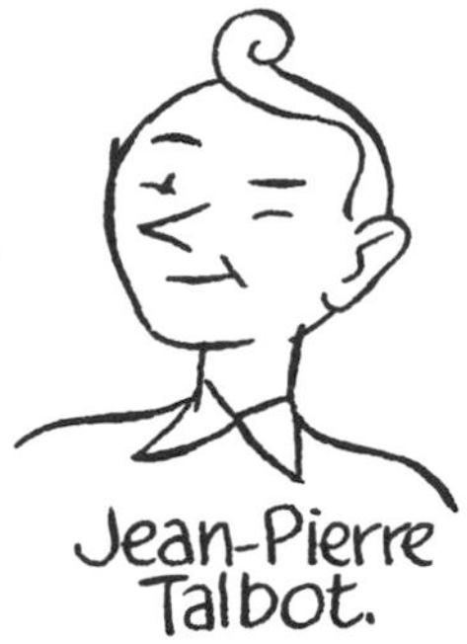
Jean-Pierre Talbot.

Talbot played the part of Tintin in the movies *The Mystery of the Golden Fleece* and *The Blue Oranges*, with Georges Wilson and Jean Bouise as Captain Haddock. He was never to appear in a feature film again. Off-screen, the incarnation of Tintin eventually became a teacher and lost his hair.

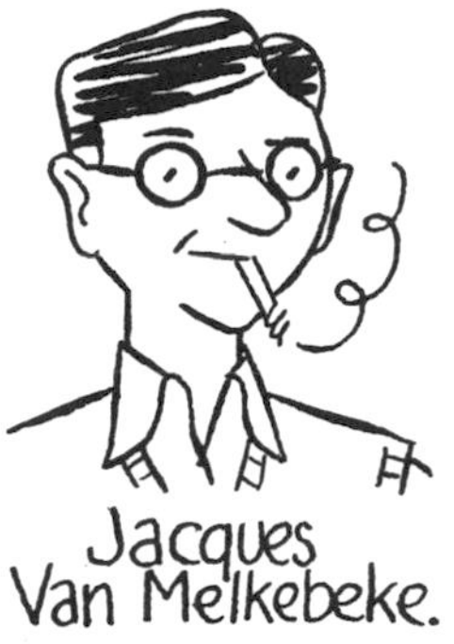
Jacques Van Melkebeke.

Painter and art critic, Jacques wrote for the Belgian daily newspaper *Le Soir* during the German occupation. He became friends with Georges, who was also a regular contributor to the newspaper, and together they co-wrote the play *Tintin in India, The Mystery of the Blue Diamond*. When the magazine *Le Journal de Tintin* was launched, Georges pressured Leblanc to accept Van Melkebeke as chief editor. But the ex-journalist could not escape his recent past and a police raid of the magazine's offices put an end to his appointment. Hiding in Georges's shadow, Van Melkebeke contributed to several Tintin adventures, including the two moon books.

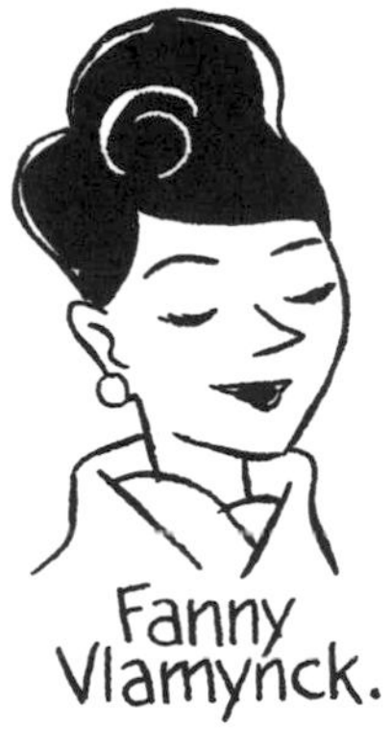
Fanny Vlamynck.

Born in 1934 in Schaerbeek, she joined Hergé's studio in 1956 as a colorist. Five months later, she began an affair with Georges that would greatly alter the course of his life. Nearing fifty, he felt revitalized by this relationship. Though the pace of his work slowed, he took greater pleasure in life, finally beginning to travel and pursuing his interest in Asian philosophies. Fanny helped him leave Germaine, for whom he no longer felt more than friendly affection. When Georges experienced severe writer's block, she encouraged him to turn to psychoanalysis for help. They were married in a private wedding on May 10, 1977. Becoming heir to the copyright in 1983, she created the Fondation Hergé three years later, with the goal of ensuring the integrity, longevity, and management of Georges's work.

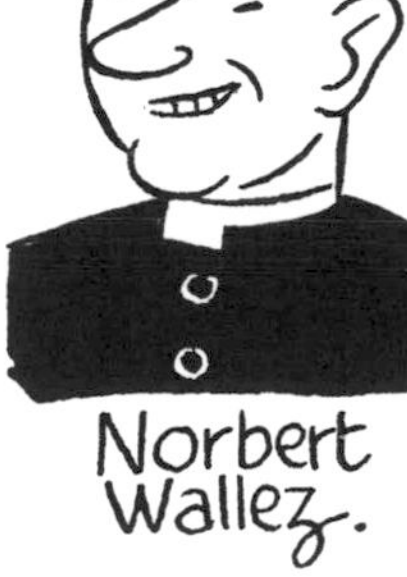
Norbert Wallez.

Born in 1882, Father Norbert Wallez, "the combative priest," ruled with an iron fist over the daily paper *XXe Siècle*. A virulent polemicist (an ideologue fueled by the caustic arguments of the Action Française and Charles Maurras), a zealous admirer of Mussolini, and hostile to Jews, Bolsheviks, Freemasons, and parliamentary democracy, this ultra-Catholic, who helped launch the career of Léon Degrelle and was referred to by his enemies

as a "fascist of the first order," played a key role in the life of Georges. A cultivated non-conformist and truculent bon vivant, he encouraged his protégé to abandon his natural dilettantism and seek perfection. Having brought him on board as the illustrator of the *XXe Siècle*'s literary supplement, in 1928 he put Georges in charge of the *Petit XXe*, a weekly children's feature that launched Tintin's career. Forever marked by the moral and intellectual influence of Father Wallez, Georges gradually withdrew from his ideological grip but remained a loyal friend throughout the Father's fall from grace after the war and until his death in 1952.

Georges visited the American artist during a trip to New York. "Hergé influenced my work as much as Disney," the prince of pop art would say. To celebrate his marriage with Fanny, Georges's friends gave him a portrait of himself by Warhol. Created by the Factory, this four-paneled serigraph, based on a Polaroid, cost them $70,000.

Andy Warhol.

Bookseller at the Librairie Coloniale bookstore in Ixelles, scoutmaster of the Saint-Boniface troop in which Georges distinguished himself as a senior patrol leader under the totem name Curious Fox, and district commissioner of the Belgian Catholic Scouts for the region of Brussels, René Weverbergh was also the editor of the magazine *Le Boy-Scout*. Weverbergh recognized Georges's talent early on, publishing drawings Georges made in 1922, and in 1926, his first serialized story, *Les Extraordinaires Aventures de Totor C.P. des Hannetons*. Upon Weverbergh's recommendation, Father Wallez hired the young man to join the Société Nouvelle Presse et Librairie, publisher of the newspaper *XXe Siècle*. Georges held various minor positions at the newspaper before launching his true career in 1927, following his return from military service.

René Weverbergh.

BIBLIOGRAGHY

30X40 — Joost Swarte, Futuropolis 1981

The Andy Warhol Diaries — Andy Warhol, Warner Books 1989

Bob de Moor — Pierre-Yves Bourdil and Bernard Tordeur, Lombard 1986

Casterman, Deux Cents Ans d'Edition et d'Imprimerie — Casterman 1980

Les Châtelains de Laeken — Gerty Colins, Presses de la Cité 1984

Dictionnaire Mondial de la Bande Dessinée — Patrick Gaumer and Cloude Moliterni, Larousse 1994

L'Ecole d'Hergé — François Rivière, Glénat 1976

Entretiens avec Hergé — Numa Sadoul, Casterman 1989

E.P. Jacobs, 30 Ans de Bandes Dessinées — Alain Littaye, Comic Sentinel 1973

L'Esprit Zen — Alan Watts, Dangles 1990

Goscinny — Marie-Ange Guillaum and José-Louis Bocquet, Actes Sud 1997

Hergé — Pierre Assouline, Plon 1996

Hergé — Benoît Peeters, Éditions Décembre 1983

Hergé, Correspondance — Edith Allaert and Jacques Bertin, Duculot 1989

Hergé et Tintin, Reporters — Philippe Goddin, Lombard 1986

Hergé, les Débuts d'un Illustrateur — Benoît Peeters, Casterman 1987

Hergé, Portrait Biographique — Thierry Smoldere and Pierre Sterckx, Casterman 1988

Hergé, Tintin le Terrible ou l'Alphabet des Riches — Alain Bonfand and Jean-Luc Marion, Hachette Livre 1996

Histoire du Journal Tintin — Alain Lerman, Glénat 1979

Le Monde d'Hergé — Benoît Peeters, Casterman 1983

Un Opéra de Papier — Edgar de Recherche Graphique, Magic Strip 1981

Tracé R.G. — Huibrecht Van Opstal, Lefrancq 1998

José-Louis Bocquet is a French novelist, journalist, and essayist. He has written more than twenty books, including biographies of other cartooning legends such as René Goscinny (Astérix) and Yves Chaland. *Jean-Luc Fromental* is the author of more than thirty French graphic novels. He has collaborated with many key figures in French comics, including Yves Chaland and Blexbolex. *Stanislas Barthélémy* has drawn graphic novels and children's books in France since 1986. He is one of the founding members of the seminal French publishing house L'Association.

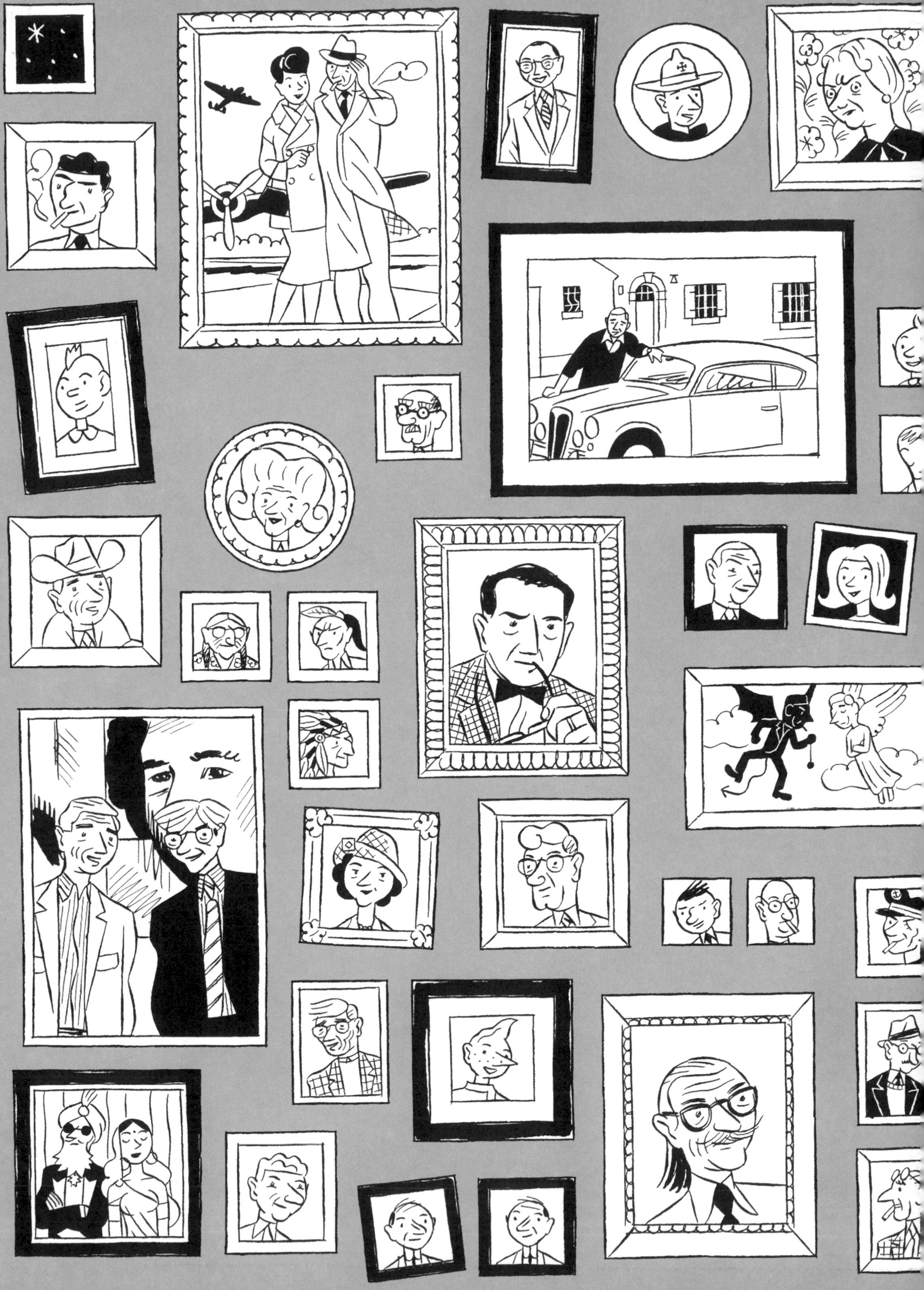